ACHIEVING YOUR
Divine
POTENTIAL

ACHIEVING YOUR
Divine
POTENTIAL

Become All You Were Created to Be

BISHOP JIM LOWE

Bridge-Logos
Orlando, Florida 32822 USA

Bridge-Logos

Orlando, Florida 32822 USA

Achieving Your Divine Potential
Become All You Were Created to Be
by Bishop Jim Lowe

Library of Congress Card Catalog Number: 2007928782
ISBN: 978-088270-205-6

Printed in the United States of America.

All scriptural quotes, unless otherwise noted, are from The HOLY BIBLE, NEW INTERNATIONAL VERSION. Copyright 1973, 1978, 1984 by International Bible Society. Used by permission of Zondervan Publishing House. All rights reserved.

Scripture quotations identified as KJV are from the *King James Version* of the Bible. Scripture quotations identified as NKJV are from the *New King James Version* of the Bible.

Please note that the author's style capitalizes certain pronouns in Scripture that refer to the Father, Son, and Holy Spirit, and may differ from some Bible publishers' styles.

Take note that the name of satan and related names are not capitalized. We choose not to acknowledge him even to the point of violating grammatical rules.

G616.316.N.m706.35240

Contents

Foreword

What Potential Is

Potential is defined as that which is possible, but not yet realized. It is something that possesses the ability or the likelihood of occurring. I'm sure you are already aware of potential with regard to your life. For instance, newborns have the potential of walking within the first two years of their lives. Some babies don't begin to walk during that stage, but most will; therefore, we understand that the potential of a child learning to walk by the age of two is very high.

An individual goes to school to improve his or her potential for success in life. For example, a student who studies pre-law has the potential to go on to law school. Once he or she completes law school, the student has the potential to pass the bar examination and then become a lawyer. A person who invests in certain stocks does so in the belief that the stocks possess the potential to provide him or her with certain financial returns. An airplane that is parked in a hangar has the potential to fly. In each case potential is realized when certain conditions are met.

God has deposited natural potential within every person. All of us are given special abilities and specific talents to enable us to work through our problems, meet challenges, and find answers and solutions. For instance, some persons are born with the potential for great athletic ability, while others enter life with a potential for the sciences or arts. Then there are some who possess a particular potential for compassion, caring, and giving high regard to others. Even with all this God-given potential, however, we are destined to fall short of our true potential because we are innately limited as human beings.

We're limited by the laws of nature—time, space, and matter—and the world with its unforeseen circumstances and trials. We are limited by relationships, a lack of resources, our outlook on things, our health, and so many other things. Our efforts are often misdirected in pursuits that aren't suited for us. As a consequence of misdirection and time wasted in dead-end pursuits, many of us are still underdeveloped and fall far short of what our true capabilities are.

In spite of our limitations, there is a far greater potential available to us. Its power and our ability to acquire it are clearly defined in the Word of God.

What Is *Divine Potential*?

Divine potential is the untapped, God-given ability that is available to you to assist God in fulfilling His purposes on earth. It is your ability to overcome mediocrity, emptiness, and areas of defeat or constant struggle and to reach the fulfillment that is provided for you by God. It is the potential of God's presence and power working in you that can make all things possible.

Divine potential has been given to and awaits the acceptance of those who are willing to participate in it. It is the power of Almighty God to alter the fundamental laws of the universe in order to accomplish His purposes through earthen vessels. The Apostle Peter spoke of it when he said:

> *His divine power has given us everything we need for life and godliness through our knowledge of him who called us by his own glory and goodness. Through these he has given us his very great and precious promises, so that through them you may participate in the divine nature and escape the corruption in the world caused by evil desires* (2 Peter 1:3-4).

As you study this work, you will realize that Almighty God is willing to invest His potential and divine power in you. His divine power works with, for, and within you to develop all He has purposed for your life. When it is developed, His divine potential is of immense value and infinite force. He directs your steps to greatness in this life and in the world to come. As a result, you experience great eternal rewards. His plans come to pass in your life as you do all that's required of you.

You are His child and He withholds no good thing from you when you are submitted to Him. It is God's pleasure to give you His Kingdom in this life—in the here and now. It is His will for you to experience His divine power working in you and accomplishing His purposes. All you have to do is accept it.

You have been created by God to exceed your own and others' expectations of you. You are created to do the supernatural for the glory of God. God does not fail. The potential He has placed within you is certain and it guarantees your success. You can do all things through Christ who strengthens you to accomplish it. (See Philippians 4:13.)

God does not fail, and His Word will never change. It will remain the same forever.

> *The grass withers and the flowers fall, but the word of our God stands forever* (Isaiah 40:8).

The scripture states, *"My people are destroyed from lack of knowledge"* (Hosea 4:6). Sadly, because many are not knowledgeable of their divine potential, they limit their growth and development and forfeit their covenant rights that have been granted to them by their faith in Christ. They deprive their families and communities of the wonderful benefits they could provide for them. Furthermore, an inability to recognize divine potential may actually cause a person to become a burden and to diminish what their families and communities have gained.

Just as God spoke to a nonexistent universe and it came into being, God has spoken words over you that have given you immense power—power to alter and control your environment, power to excel and not fail and power to do great exploits in the earth. We have a choice to either accept or deny what God has spoken over us. This choice is unique to humans. Other creatures were created by the command of God without the option to make choices. Therefore, what God said to this vast universe was without challenge and His will was done immediately.

In Genesis 1:26-28 we read God's life-giving words with regard to us:

> *Then God said, "Let us make man **in our image**, in our likeness, and let them rule over the fish of the sea and the birds of the air, over the livestock, over all the earth, and over all the creatures that move along the ground." So God created man in his own image, in the image of God he created him; male and female he created them. **God blessed them** and said to them, "**Be fruitful** and **increase in number; fill the earth** and **subdue it. Rule over** the fish of the sea and the birds of the air and over every living creature that moves on the ground."* (Emphasis mine.)

These words, which have been read time and time again by so many, lay the foundation for our triumphant work in life. In this Scripture, we see God empowering human beings and giving them divine directives for their lives. God gives human beings immeasurable potential, a potential that is bound only by the limitations we accept by choice.

I'm sure you've heard these clichés: "What the mind of man can conceive, can be achieved." "Where there's a will, there's a way." "If you believe, all things are possible." All these things *are* true only when God is with you. If you believe God and apply His principles correctly, what used to be simply clichés will begin to manifest as reality.

Consider the miraculous things that were done by the men and women of the Bible. Remember, God is no respecter of persons. He honors those who honor Him. He dwells with anyone who receives Him and exercises His divine power. The potential is there. It's divine. And it's for *you!*

God has predestined a specific vision and mission for your life. I can't tell you what your specific mission in life is, but I can show you how to become aware of it. Then, once you have knowledge of it, I can help you seize your divine potential so that you may use it to become all God intended for you to be. As you apply the principles that are detailed in this book, you'll develop your faith in God and increase your capacity to participate in His *". . . divine nature and escape the corruption in the world caused by evil desires"* (2 Peter 1:4).

You will develop your faith by:

- Finding from the Word of God the true revelation of who you are
- Recognizing God's basic commands for a blessed, fruitful life
- Discovering who God created you to be
- Learning to see things as they are and as they should be
- Uncovering and utilizing the forces available to change your life
- Recognizing what you can become in Christ Jesus
- Resolving to renew your mind to live your life to the maximum
- Developing a plan to become what God says you can become
- Following the plan God has given you with diligence

As you read this book, my prayer is that the Holy Spirit will speak to you through the words you read and reveal more to you than what is written herein. I pray that He will make it personal to you. I know God loves you and desires for you to live a blessed life. You are His child and He cares for you. He gave all of us His divine potential. It awaits you; seize it!

INTRODUCTION

The Ultimate Partnership

Living for God's Purpose

"Before I formed you in the womb I knew you" (Jeremiah 1:5).

These are the words God spoke to Jeremiah to let him know He had a plan for his life. They are a revelation for all humanity to understand. Our lives did not begin in our mothers' wombs. We existed before conception, and we were known by God from the beginning. He had a relationship with us, and He knew each one of us by name. Then, when the Almighty deemed it appropriate, He released our spirit to come to the earth. As He did with Jeremiah, He gave a purpose and mission to everyone. He has predestined you according to His plan so that you would fulfill His purpose.

There are no worthless people in God's creation. He has given everyone a divine potential to do supernatural exploits that bring glory to His name. When you fall short of this potential, you deprive yourself and your family of the optimum life-style that was planned for you and them. You also deprive your generation and the world of your unique gifts that were given by God to bless mankind. God has chosen you and made you extraordinary and special. Therefore, you have tremendous value.

No matter what you think of yourself, you're no accident! You are God's creation, and you were born to be a blessing to those

1

who are around you. When you set yourself in agreement with His purpose for your life, you walk in the power of God, which manifests in supernatural acts in your life. It is for this cause that you were born—not for yourself, but for His purpose and His plans. When these truths become evident to you, you will experience a peace and sense of fulfillment that will cause you to begin each day with confidence and end each day with satisfaction.

The Bible, the most widely read book ever, details God's revelation of himself to mankind. As the Creator and Author of all things, both seen and unseen, He also reveals His divine plan for mankind. Though people may consider themselves to be the masters of their own destiny, God is still the Owner of this world and universe, and He will ultimately see His will fulfilled. Throughout the pages of the Bible we see God manifesting himself in countless, miraculous ways in order to bring His purposes to pass. There are times when we see Him acting independently; for example, in the creation of the world, the sending of the great flood, the confusion of the tongues at Babel, the tearing of the veil of the Temple, and most importantly, the raising of Jesus from the tomb.

However, in the majority of the biblical narratives, we see God doing the miraculous principally in cooperation with a person who allows Him to work through him or her on His behalf. God works with people because God gave dominion over the earth to them in the very beginning. Therefore, people have control over the earth and can do with it as they see fit—either for good or for bad. For the time being, God has chosen not to violate the authority He has granted to people, because He respects His own Word, which He gave to us in the beginning. Psalms 115:16 is one of the many Scriptures that confirm this: *"The highest heavens belong to the Lord, but the earth he has given to man."*

This is like the owner of a business who hires several managers to assist him in developing the business. He gives each manager authority and control over a certain area and defines specific goals or objectives for him or her to accomplish. The owner sees to it that each manager has all of the basic tools and materials that are necessary. He then leaves it up to each manager to accomplish his stated objectives. If the owner wishes to implement changes in an operation under the control of a manager, he will instruct the manager and then assist him or her as needed in order to accomplish it. He does not undertake a certain action in a specific department without first informing the manager of that department, even though he certainly has every right to do so. He respects the position of his appointed manager. It is only when a manager continuously fails to accomplish his objectives that the owner reasserts his full authority.

This is the way God deals with people. As the Owner of all things, He has given each of us authority and management over certain areas of His earth. He has also given us the basic tools and materials that are necessary to accomplish His assigned goals and objectives. Because He has given us authority, He hesitates to override the authority He gives unless it is absolutely necessary. Instead, He works alongside us, His managers. It is, therefore, up to us to make certain that we understand His objectives and take the necessary actions to accomplish all we have been instructed to do. We can be confident that He has not given us any assignments that we cannot accomplish, and if we need His assistance, we can count on His support. All we have to do is ask. We are His workmanship, and He is giving us the opportunity to complete His work in the earth. Because this is so, we should be truly honored.

In Ezekiel 22:30 we read this statement: *"I looked for a man among them who would build up the wall and stand before me in the gap on behalf of the land so I would not have to destroy it, but I found none."* In 1 Corinthians 3:9 we read, *"We are laborers together with God"* (KJV). These scriptures, as well as many others, indicate that God expends effort to find individuals who are willing to do His bidding so that He may work through them.

In 2 Chronicles 16:9 we read another very exciting and most revealing scripture: *"For the eyes of the Lord range throughout the earth to strengthen those whose hearts are fully committed to him."* Here we learn that God will contribute His power to assist us when our hearts are devoted and committed to Him. This simple thought is a biblical law that is repeated throughout the Bible. Remember what Jesus said in Matthew 6:33: *"But seek first his kingdom and his righteousness, and all these things will be given to you as well."* The promise is that God will give to us all that we need for life if we will simply focus on accomplishing His purposes.

Be strong and very courageous. Be careful to obey all the law my servant Moses gave you; do not turn from it to the right or to the left, that you may be successful wherever you go. Do not let this Book of the Law depart from your mouth; meditate on it day and night, so that you may be careful to do everything written in it. Then you will be prosperous and successful (Joshua 1:7-8).

God does not lie. If He promises something, He will bring it to pass. He promises that if our hearts and actions honor Him, He will honor us with His power working through us.

"For God does not show favoritism" (Romans 2:11).

God does not show favoritism because of a person's class, income, race, status, or any of the criteria by which we judge each other. God will do things for all. What He has done for one, He will do for another. He is simply looking for those who will respect and honor His Word above all things.

Noah, for example, was a man who was righteous in God's sight. He placed God's priorities above his own. As a result, God revealed to him that He was going to bring a massive flood over all the earth. God then instructed Noah to build a massive ship that the world had never seen before. It took Noah over 100 years to construct the ark. When it was completed, God brought the animals to Noah and had them board the ship. You know the rest of the story. It rained for forty days and forty nights. All mankind and all the animals that lived on the land were destroyed, with the exception of Noah and all those who were aboard the ark. Noah was fulfilling his divine potential by allowing God to work through him to fulfill His purposes on the earth.

Consider the familiar story of David and Goliath. David was a mere shepherd boy. However, God invested divine potential for greatness within him. When Samuel was looking for a candidate to be king over Israel, he had David's father present his sons before him so that God might select one of them to be king. Neither David's father nor his brothers saw anything in David that would make him worthy to be considered for this important position. Therefore, he was not even included in the selection process. When Samuel prepared to select one of David's brothers, however, God stopped him and told him that he was not the one that He had selected. He explained to Samuel that man looks at the outward appearance, but God sees all that is on the inside of a person. David was chosen above all his brothers and was anointed by Samuel, God's representative, to be king.

In this story we see that true greatness is not always readily apparent. It is what is in the heart of a person that matters. God said that David was a man after His own heart. And it is because of David's desire to please God that God chose him to do great exploits in His name.

David was not even considered to be a warrior when he went to the battlefield to carry greetings to his brothers. It was there that he heard the giant Goliath challenge Saul's army, and David grew disturbed. Not only were Goliath's words insulting to Saul and his army, but in David's mind, he was defying the armies of the living God. David had such a high regard for God that he would not allow any challenge made against Him to stand. As a result, David, without shield or sword, single-handedly defeated Goliath with a sling and a single rock!

It's interesting to note that when David fought Goliath, he did not do so for his glory or for the army's sake. He told Goliath he came against him "*. . . in the name of the Lord Almighty, the God of the armies of Israel, whom you have defied*" (1 Samuel 17:45). As a result, God gave him the victory.

There are many more examples in the Bible of people who were used by God to do supernatural work. The common ingredient in each of these stories is a person's willingness to submit to God, to believe, and to act upon the Word of God that had been spoken to them. This book is about helping *you* become such a person by helping you to fulfill and accomplish your divine potential.

God Desires to Work in and Through You

God's ultimate desire is for you to be a person through whom He can work to fulfill His will. This was God's plan from the very beginning. When He created the heavens and the earth, He placed Adam in the Garden "to work it and take care of it." Now, think about this. God had just created everything. He did not need man's assistance, yet He placed him in the Garden to work it and take care of it. This reveals to us that God was allowing man to do a work He could have done himself. But His will was for man to do it. God walked and talked with this man. It was God's pleasure to have fellowship with him.

Unfortunately, the man and woman God created decided they no longer wanted to submit to His authority. They chose to experience life in a manner that was contrary to His will. By their choice they decided to do things in a manner that was different from what God had designed for them to do. They disobeyed His Word. The result of their action was that their fellowship with God was broken. He, a holy God, could no longer walk in the Garden with the man and woman who had rebelled against Him.

Since that time, God has sought to reestablish open fellowship with the sons and daughters of the first man. He inspired the entire Bible in which He detailed His desires for us. Seeking an unhindered relationship with His people, God selected a single man, Abraham, and built a nation out of his sons and daughters. When He appeared to Moses in the form of a burning bush, He was seeking to free a nation of people He could call His own. When Moses submitted himself to do His will, God created extraordinary, supernatural events through him so that He might have a nation of people through whom He could work. God was not satisfied to exist on the earth in a burning bush, so He told the people to make a tabernacle that would allow Him to dwell among them. However, God was not satisfied to have His relationship with His people confined to a tabernacle and, later, a temple.

In the course of time God sent His Son, Jesus, to pay the penalty for the rebellion of humanity against Him. Jesus came to reestablish the ability of the common man to have a relationship with God. God would again be able to dwell within the hearts of the people He had created and to have fellowship and a personal relationship with them. His people would then be able to assist Him in fulfilling His purposes on earth.

God still has plans for human beings. He still has things He would like to do in the earth. The world that exists now is not the world that God wanted for us in the beginning. Therefore, God is constantly seeking men and women who will submit themselves to Him so that He might do the great works in them that He did in biblical times. He has stated throughout the Bible that He will involve himself in the affairs of people, and He has confirmed His Word with signs and miracles to prove it.

Today, however, we're conditioned by the world's doctrine to believe that God no longer operates in the same ways He did in biblical times. Many think that the time of miracles and the supernatural has passed. Yet God never changes. He is the same yesterday, today, and tomorrow. (See Hebrews 13:8.)

Think about this. If God never changes, and He is the same God today as He was in biblical times, why isn't He performing the great signs and wonders He performed then? I propose to you that He hasn't changed at all. *We have*!

The Nazareth Negation

Let's take a look now at another biblical event. It happened in a small town called Nazareth, Jesus' hometown. He had grown up there and the people knew Him. They knew His parents. They remembered Him growing up as a young boy. Although Jesus had done a great many miracles elsewhere, the Bible says that in this city He couldn't do any, except heal a few sick people. (See Mark 6:5.)

The people of Nazareth spent their time questioning what Jesus did and the wisdom behind what He said rather than trusting and believing in Him. Because he was a "local" and they knew Him to be the son of a simple carpenter, they thought He didn't have authority. The Bible says they were, in fact, offended. This attitude of questioning and offense caused a lack of faith that hindered Jesus' ability to act on their behalf. He was still full of power and had the ability to do just as many miraculous works there for them as he had done elsewhere for others.

Lack of faith that hinders God's work has profound implications for us. I call this the **Nazareth Negation.** When people join together and come to a consensus that God does not perform miracles, their combined lack of faith has a profoundly negative impact on God's performance. Remember, God listens to people. If they believe that He will not perform a miracle, He will not!

Our lack of faith can also negate His power to act for our benefit. If we don't truly know the God of the Bible and create a limited "god of our own choosing" or believe that He doesn't do miracles anymore, we negate His miraculous power and keep it from working through us and for us. And then, if we do see the works of His hands, we seek ways to explain them away as chance occurrences or coincidences and thereby dismiss the possibility of future occurrences.

God respects His own Word and honors the authority He has given to us—especially the authority to choose our personal destiny. He, therefore, allows us the power to negate His will for our lives.

Now some might say that this ability and faith for God to act does not apply to the ability to affect the physical environment or material things. Why, then, did Jesus calm the wind, still the waves, raise the dead, and then tell us that we would do even greater things than these? Why would He mislead us? How was it that Moses parted the Red Sea and Joshua stopped the sun and caused the walls of Jericho to fall? Why would God allow such things to happen if they were not to serve as examples of what could be done through faith? If these things cannot be done and they have passed away, why would He deceive us into thinking nothing is impossible if we believe? Why would He say such "misleading" things as, *"If you believe, you will receive whatever you ask for in prayer?"* (Matthew 21:22)

He said these things to let us know that He does the supernatural in our lives when we simply have faith to believe in Him. When we overcome our unbelief and focus on and believe what God says, we see the supernatural manifest in our lives and in our own time just as it was manifested in days of old. God has not changed! We just believe He has, and our lack of faith negates God's power in our lives.

Don't Negate!

God still has plans for us! He is looking for those who are fully committed to Him so that He might strengthen them to do His work. (See 2 Chronicles 16:9.)

God has given me a passion to help you become the complete person He desires for you to be and to fulfill your divine potential. My goal is for you to know and seize it—through knowledge of the Word of God. I seek to move you away from accepting a common life that is subject to the world's limitations and to ignite in you a desire to strive to achieve the impossible and reach the unattainable. I want to create in you a craving to become a person who appeals to God so that He may choose you, just as he chose Noah and other great men and women, so that He may work in you supernaturally to accomplish His purposes. I want you to become a lightning rod for the power of God so that His power will flow through you and you will become a blessing to mankind.

God has given you the divine potential to excel. You were created in His image and, therefore, you should have an attitude of success and gain. You were created to prosper in whatever you commit your hands to do. God has given you all you need for this moment, for this opportunity, and for the future ahead. The only thing you have to do is tap into it by believing God for it. Victory is waiting for you!

When you fully understand that God has instilled divine potential in you, and that there's a power working within you to achieve God's plan for your life, then you begin to do great works.

So let's begin!

CHAPTER 1

The Revelation of
Your Divine Potential

Now Is Your Time for a New Beginning!

Throughout this process, it's important to allow God to order your footsteps. Listen to Him and hear what He is saying to you. You must remember and constantly be aware that God created this universe with the words He spoke. What He says is powerful and it will have a tremendous impact upon your life if you respond appropriately. Jesus said:

> *"Consider carefully what you hear," he continued. "With the measure you use, it will be measured to you—and even more"* (Mark 4:24).

What we hear affects our knowledge of things. Our knowledge affects our thinking. Our thinking affects the choices we make. The choices we make affect our lives. It all begins with what we hear.

Consider this: If we truly hear—I mean really hear with understanding—what God says about us, we will think about what He has said. Then we will make choices based upon what He has said about us; our decisions will be based upon His Word. He has stated that His Word shall not fail. Thus any decisions based upon His Word will come to pass. His Word cannot fail because God will back up what He has said. In fact, He has stated that Heaven and earth will pass away before His Word does. Therefore, what God says about us, it is truth. It cannot fail!

It was His plan, before you were born, to see you fully manifest your divine potential and do great things in His name! He is the Author, Developer, and Finisher of what you can and will become. He has even promised that He will help you fulfill your divine potential.

> " ... for it is God who works in you to will and to act according to his good purpose" (Philippians 2:13).

Do you see the power of those words? God works in us and causes us to *want* to do what He has called us to do. Psalm 37:4 says, *"Delight yourself in the Lord and he will give you the desires of your heart."* As your heart is devoted to Him, He will give you the desire, willingness, and passion to do His will. Then as He tells us, in Philippians 2:13, that He will work in us to bring to pass the purpose that He has for our lives. We must allow Him to affect our will and act in us to accomplish His purpose. He will do that through the words He speaks over us.

Consider what the Lord said to Jeremiah when He announced His divine plans for him:

> *Before I formed you in the womb I knew you, before you were born I set you apart; I appointed you as a prophet to the nations* (Jeremiah 1:5).

What He said about Jeremiah is also true of you. Now think about that!

The God who spoke the universe into existence had just spoken to this man about his divine potential. All Jeremiah had to do was to accept what God was saying about him, believe it, and act on it. Instead, his reaction was one of doubt:

> *I do not know how to speak; I am only a child* (Jeremiah 1:6).

Being doubtful is fully understandable when things are considered in "the natural." His argument might have been based on past experiences, comparisons, or others' comments about him, but notice the flaw in his logic. He declared that the Almighty God was incompetent and incapable of understanding the situation. Jeremiah was looking at who he was and his limitations, instead of who God was.

Like Jeremiah, you may be looking at your situation to determine whether or not you will believe God. If so, you must stop looking at things from your perspective and start looking at them from God's position. Stop trying to do things according to your ability; instead, do them according to God's ability in you. Remember who Almighty God is and the power of His Words.

God understood Jeremiah's apprehension and He understands ours. He declared to Jeremiah:

> *Do not say, "I am only a child." You must go to everyone I send you to and say whatever I command you. Do not be afraid of them, <u>for I am with you</u> and will rescue you* (Jeremiah 1:7-8, emphasis mine).

You see, God formed and set Jeremiah apart in the womb particularly for this purpose. Jeremiah didn't need to be concerned. God said that He would be with him and meet his every need. Therefore, he would lack nothing he needed to accomplish what God had called him to.

Then our loving, encouraging Lord reached out His hand, touched Jeremiah's mouth, and said,

> *Now, I have put my words in your mouth. See, today I appoint you over nations and kingdoms to uproot and tear down, to destroy and overthrow, to build and to plant* (Jeremiah 1:9-10).

Recognize now what God did. He revealed to Jeremiah by His words the specific mission and plan He had for his life. All Jeremiah had to do was believe and act with confidence, knowing God would do as He said. As Jeremiah obeyed God's command, God would complete and fulfill whatever he seemed to lack at the moment when Jeremiah needed it.

God also has prearranged strategic points in your life and given you a fresh supply of His anointing to enable you to handle any situation or circumstance you might encounter. When you're on the course God intends for you, the necessary supplies and resources will be there to enable you to acquire and seize your divine potential.

Yet, you say you do not see God's provision now. Why? Where is it? When you reach the right place at the proper time, God will reveal the provision to you. You won't see the supplies and resources until you begin believing in the vision, speaking the vision, and acting out the vision. You have to learn to see what *God* wants you to see before you will see what *you* want to see. As you learn to seek God and His purposes for your life, then you'll see the provision.

God reveals things to you and then waits for your response. He expects you to believe and proclaim the things He has shown to you. To understand this more clearly, let's return to Jeremiah. God wanted him to see and to speak what he saw, so the Lord asked,

> *"What do you see, Jeremiah?" "I see the branch of an almond tree," I replied. The LORD said to me, "You have seen correctly, for I am watching to see that my word is fulfilled"* (Jeremiah 1:11-12).

I was puzzled when I first read this verse and did some research to find out what it meant. I learned that most plants and trees blossom in the spring, but the almond tree doesn't. It blossoms in February and March, before most of the other plants do. So, when everything around it looks dead, the almond tree comes to life!

Everything around Jeremiah could have been sick or dead, but the Lord promised Jeremiah that He would watch over His spoken Word to bring it about, even when things seemed doubtful or uncertain. All Jeremiah had to do was accept what God said and allow God to work through him. God would provide assurance for the concerns that kept Jeremiah from believing and acting on His Word. In this way, God guaranteed that Jeremiah would accomplish the purpose He had planned for his life.

Just as He did with Jeremiah, God will speak to you and explain His plan for your life. The situation or task at hand might seem to be or even actually be impossible to everyone else around you, but when God is with you and in you, you'll blossom when others can't, no matter how difficult the circumstances may be. God supplies the necessary provisions every step of the way. His Word will come to pass in your life. You don't have to worry about how or when. All you have to do is to trust God and obey Him.

Compare yourself to Jeremiah. He first doubted God. However, he heard what God had to say, learned to trust God, and fulfilled his divine potential—just as you will! Maybe you are thinking, "How can I compare myself to Jeremiah? He was a man who was chosen of God, a prophet who wrote his own book, which is found in the holy Bible. He had a purpose to speak to the nations and write the scriptures."

You have also been chosen. Your misgivings and arguments might sound logical to the "natural" person because they are patterned after this world. Through ages of worldly thoughts and fleshly dominance, we have fallen into the accepted customs, cycles, and limitations of every age and era. We have limited ourselves and denied our true divine potential.

The world is not your friend, and it will always try to keep you from knowing and achieving your divine potential. Therefore, God tells you to stop allowing the world to set your limitations. We must learn to look to God and His Word. His Word never fails!

> *Do not conform any longer to the pattern of this world, but be transformed by the renewing of your mind. Then you will be able to test and approve what God's will is—his good, pleasing and perfect will* (Romans 12:2).

You must allow yourself to be transformed by His Word, which is the agent of your transformation. You do not have to make it happen; just let it happen. Remember, you have a free will. God desires to use His Word to transform your life. He will not force you. His Word created the universe and transformed a willing Jeremiah. His Word can also transform you. Will you let Him do it?

Maximized Divine Potential in Christ

The Bible reveals that the Old Testament was merely *"... a shadow of the good things that are coming—not the realities themselves"* (Hebrews 10:1). It explains, *"... Jesus has become the guarantee of a better covenant"* (Hebrews 7:22). There were great men and women who lived under the first covenant, but even greater potential exists for people since Christ has come. The opportunity has been restored by Christ Jesus for you to achieve your divine potential under the New Covenant established by Him. I must say emphatically that you cannot achieve your divine potential without the power of Christ working in you!

You must be born again of the Spirit of God, for the Holy Spirit is the force that gives you the power to achieve your divine potential. Your divine potential cannot be reached in any other way. You cannot even see the potential that is available to you unless His Holy Spirit gives you the insight.

Now let us take a look at the plan of God. In the beginning, all things He created were in perfect harmony with His way of doing things. Unfortunately, the first man, Adam, chose another way that destroyed the perfect relationship that God had with him. The result was that man could no longer walk in perfect communion with God. Man had chosen to listen to the serpent instead.

Adam's failure to trust God and to do as God said resulted in sin. God, the Creator and Master of the universe, could not tolerate rebellion against Him. As it is with the governments of nations, any rebellion against a sovereign king, nation, or government is considered treason. Treason is punishable by death. Such was the case as a result of man's rebellion against God, and such treason is sin. The punishment for this treason against God's Kingdom is also death.

The consequences of Adam's action were that death entered the world and death was transferred from the first man, and it then became the inheritance of all mankind. Death was a result of man's rebellion against God. Every person who came after Adam was also guilty of treason and, therefore, everyone deserves the penalty of death.

The connection between man and God was severed. As a result, people have encountered resistance whenever they've attempted to accomplish things in the earth, and this has caused much distress and discomfort for humanity. When man's relationship with God was severed, the door was opened for potential failure.

The errors of Adam and Eve are being repeated every day. For some reason most of us would rather learn from what we can hear or see from the world than to accept what we have heard from the mouth of God. We were created to gain knowledge from the Word of God first and then to learn from our environment. Adam and Eve reversed this process. This reversal has made mankind subject to the domination of the world's systems and devices.

> *We all, like sheep, have gone astray, each of us has turned to his own way; and the Lord has laid on him the iniquity of us all* (Isaiah 53:6).

We have all sought to get away from the leadership of God and do things the way we want to do them. Romans 3: 23 says: " ... *for all have sinned and fall short of the glory of God.*" This clearly means that everyone is guilty of rebellion against God and deserves the penalty of death.

Again, this was not God's desire from the beginning, but man's action did not take God by surprise. He had a plan from the very creation of the world that would provide a way for man to be restored to the original perfect relationship with himself. It is through the redemptive action of Christ Jesus that our perfect relationship with God is restored, giving us access to divine potential.

John 3:16 tells us: *"For God so loved the world that he gave his one and only Son, that whoever believes in him shall not perish but have eternal life."* This is reaffirmed in Romans 5:8: " ... *God demonstrates his own love for us in this: While we were still sinners, Christ died for us."* Thus, God sent His one and only Son into the world that we might live through Him and experience life abundantly. (See John 10:10.)

God made a great sacrifice in sending His Son, Jesus. The truth of the matter is that God himself came into the world to reestablish the perfect relationship with us. Therefore, Jesus made this statement, *"I and the Father are one"* (John 10: 30). He also said, *"I am the way and the truth and the life. No one comes to the Father except through me"* (John 14:6).

People are still continuously trying to find ways around Christ and trying to please God in ways they desire and concoct. But no matter what people may attempt to do on their own, they will still commit sin, and the wages of sin is death, but the gift that God supplies is eternal life in Christ Jesus our Lord. (See Romans 6:23.) Now and forever, there is only one way, and that one way is through Christ.

Now, because people have a freedom of choice, each of us has the opportunity to choose the way of God and have the perfect relationship with Him restored. Anyone who has accepted Christ is a new creation. The old is gone and the new has come. God has reconciled us to himself through Christ, not counting our sins against us. And then He gave us the message of reconciliation to give to the world. We are, therefore, Christ's ambassadors, as though God were making His appeal through us. (See 2 Corinthians 5:17-20.) God has chosen us to fulfill His work in the earth, a work that He started in Christ Jesus.

A choice has been set before you, as it was with the nation of Israel. We see in Deuteronomy 30:15-16 this same promise is given to us today.

> *See, I set before you today life and prosperity, death and destruction. For I command you today to love the Lord your God, to walk in his ways, and to keep his commands, decrees and laws; then you will live and increase, and the Lord your God will bless you in the land you are entering to possess.*

God promises us the opportunity to experience the divine potential He has prepared for us.
The choice is up to us.

> *But if serving the Lord seems undesirable to you, then choose for yourselves this day whom you will serve, whether the gods your forefathers served beyond the River, or the gods of the Amorites, in whose land you are living. But as for me and my household, we will serve the Lord* (Joshua 24:15).

The Greater Covenant

Jesus said that John the Baptist was greater than all the Old Testament prophets—Abraham, Joseph, Moses, Samuel, David, Solomon, Elijah, and others. Because of Christ, you have become a light for the world so that they will see God in you. Because you're a Christian, you have the potential to achieve greater things than all the great people of the Bible. You're a chosen part of the Kingdom of God, and you have been anointed by Christ for the work He has planned for you to do:

> *Now it is God who makes both us and you stand firm in Christ. He anointed us, set his seal of ownership on us, and put his Spirit in our hearts as a deposit, guaranteeing what is to come (2 Corinthians 1:21-22).*

Yes, we have the ability to do great things. Jesus said that we can do even greater things than the things He did because He has gone to the Father. And because of our relationship with Christ, God strengthens us. It is from Him that we have the power to accomplish any goal we set out to accomplish.

Another exciting verse of Scripture is quoted below. Compare the Word spoken here to the Word that was spoken to Jeremiah. I have taken the liberty of making this personal for you by substituting certain words:

> *Praise be to the God and Father of our Lord Jesus Christ, who has blessed us [me] in the heavenly realms with every spiritual blessing in Christ. For he chose us [me] in him before the creation of the world to be holy and blameless in his sight. In love he predestined us [me] to be adopted as his sons [children] through Jesus Christ, in accordance with his pleasure and will—to the praise of his glorious grace, which he has freely given [me] in the One he loves. In him we [I] have redemption through his blood, the forgiveness of sins, in accordance with the riches of God's grace that he lavished on us [me] with all wisdom and understanding (Ephesians 1:3-8).*

Do you get it? God has blessed you in the heavenly realms with every spiritual blessing in Christ Jesus. My brothers and sisters, you're blessed in this earth and in the heavenlies! Just like Jeremiah, you were chosen before the world began. You're called to holiness. You're God's child. You're forgiven. You're lavished with all wisdom and understanding to accomplish great exploits for the Kingdom of God and to bring blessings to your family, yourself, and God's Kingdom.

I've shown you just a few of the verses in the Bible that reveal God's will for you. As you discover more from His Word, you'll know that you have the ability to achieve your divine potential not because God is with you, but because Jesus Christ, as God, is *in* you and gives you His ability. When the odds seem against you, plant this truth in your mind. God is not just *with* you; He is *in* you!

God Will Reveal Things to You

God has promised in His Word that He will give you all you need at the exact moment you need it. You might not see the reality of what you need now for tomorrow because tomorrow has not arrived yet. But you can be certain of this: when tomorrow comes, God will be there with you, ready to supply your immediate need. Trust Him. He desires for you to be aware of your divine potential and has given you the gift of His Holy Spirit to help you understand it and your potential greatness in Him. His Spirit has even caused you to read this book so that you will develop faith for the miraculous!

Now, what does the Word say that God has prepared for you?

> However, as it is written: 'No eye has seen, no ear has heard, no mind has conceived what God has prepared for those [you] who love him'—but God has revealed it to us [you] by his Spirit. The Spirit searches all things, even the deep things of God (1 Corinthians 2:9-10).

God has given you divine potential to fulfill His predestined plan and purpose for your life, and the Spirit of God will reveal His purpose to you. Don't worry, if you desire to know it, He will not allow you to be ignorant of it. He is ready to let you know when you're ready to know. So stop turning to the world for answers and turn to God.

The world does not want you to know that you have a divine potential that was invested in you by God, and satan will do all he can to keep this information away from you. Satan knows that once you know you have divine potential and are willing to walk in it, nothing can stop you from accomplishing God's purposes. You will be an undefeatable adversary who will inflict severe and heavy casualties upon satan's kingdom. He knows there is divine potential in you, and he is tremendously afraid of your discovery of that divine potential. That is why there are so very few who are aware of it. He keeps it hidden from them, but the real truth is found in what God says;

> *"For I know the plans I have for you,"* declares the LORD, *"plans to prosper you and not to harm you, plans to give you hope and a future"* (Jeremiah 29:11).

Now, no more excuses. It's time to start looking at what you can become in Christ.

> *So from now on we regard no one from a worldly point of view. Though we once regarded Christ in this way, we do so no longer.* **Therefore, *if anyone is in Christ, he is a new creation; the old has gone, the new has come!*** (2 Corinthians 5:16-17, emphasis mine)

Understand this clearly and stop limiting God based upon your experiences and what others have said to you. You have a mandate from Almighty God, the Ruler of the universe! It can't be taken away from you. You are the master of your destiny and unless you let it go, it is yours to have forever. It can't be destroyed. God's gifts and callings are irrevocable. He will not take them back. When God said it, it was established in you and made available for you. Accept it and achieve it!

YOUR DIVINE POTENTIAL POWER POINTS!

- Potential is that which is possible, but not yet realized.
- Your divine potential is the power and presence of God within you.
- You have been given divine potential that is specific to God's purpose for your life.
- Your divine potential is maximized in Christ, as a new creation without limitation.
- The Holy Spirit will cause you to see things differently and reveal solutions to problems that others cannot solve.

A Divine Potential Prayer for You!

May the written truth in this book change the course of my life!

I ask You, Lord, to watch over Your plan for me and that Your divine potential will be seized by me through my faith and obedience to Your Word.

I pray that You will help me remove mediocrity, feelings of emptiness, failure and defeat from my life, and give me a fresh anointing of Your Spirit to know that I am more than a conqueror in Christ Jesus. Yes, Lord, bestow the abundant life You intended for me as You have stated in Your Word. I pray You will help me to know that all things are indeed possible for me because of my relationship with You. I am now confident of the manifestation of these things in Jesus' name. Amen.

CHAPTER 2

The Revelation of Your Source of Endless Empowerment

God's Image and God's Continual Blessing!

In the Book of Genesis God gave the purpose for the creation of every animal, including human beings. When God spoke, it all came to pass exactly as He said it would. Plants that had never existed came into existence. Fish that never swam began to swim. Birds that never flew began to fly. All things that God created performed as He commanded them to do.

During the creation of the heavens and the earth God gave everything to mankind: a beautifully landscaped paradise (the Garden of Eden) enveloped in eternal life and filled with precious stones, metals, food, water, and animals created just for His people. The first man, Adam, named the animals and tilled the ground. He walked in perfect fellowship with God.

In this wonderful place all Adam needed was provided for him by God. Every tree, with the exception of one, was given to him for food. He had an environment that was free from want, threat of danger, sickness, and disease. Most of all, man had eternal life in a perfect relationship with his Creator. God was willing to do everything that was best for the man He had created. This is evident by the fact that when God saw that it was not good for man to be alone, he gave him a beautiful helpmate. All man had to do was to submit to God's authority and in return, he would experience God's best forever.

Now, unlike all of the other creatures God created, man was given a freedom of choice. He had a mind that enabled him to think independently of the will of God. He was created with the unique ability to choose or reject God's Word that was spoken over him. To determine man's willingness to submit and obey Him, God planted a tree in the middle of the Garden and told him not eat of it. To further discourage him from eating the fruit of this tree, He also told him that he would die on the day he ate from the tree.

Unfortunately, the man and the woman chose badly and the consequences of this choice were devastating. As a result, God expelled the man and the woman from the Garden. In the absence of God they could no longer fulfill their divine potential.

> *Because you listened to your wife and ate from the tree about which I commanded you, 'You must not eat of it,' Cursed is the ground because of you; through painful toil you will eat of it all the days of your life. It will produce thorns and thistles for you, and you will eat the plants of the field. By the sweat of your brow you will eat your food until you return to the ground, since from it you were taken; for dust you are and to dust you will return* (Genesis 3:17-19).

Without the power of God at their disposal, all things the man and woman would try to do would now require strenuous effort. And, in the final analysis, they would experience death.

God's Original True Intention for Us

On the sixth day of creation, man was created by God and empowered with the awesome ability to take dominion over parts of His creation. Keep in mind that our God is an awesome God and we exist and live as a result of His spoken Word. What He spoke in the beginning remains true until this day. Nothing man, angels, demons, or anything else in all creation do can undo what God has spoken.

In Genesis 1:26-28 we see the truth and reality of God's spoken Word with regard to mankind in a simple phrase. Please commit these verses to memory. It is here that God stated His original purpose for the creation of man. In these few verses we see Almighty God giving man endless empowerment and a divine directive:

> *Then God said, [1] "Let us make man in our image, in our likeness, and let them rule over the fish of the sea and the birds of the air, over the livestock, over all the earth, and over all the creatures that move along the ground." So God created man in his own image, in the image of God he created him; male and female he created them. [2] God blessed them and said to them, [3] "Be fruitful and [4] increase [multiply] in number; [5] fill [replenish) the earth and [6] subdue it. [7] Rule [establish dominion] over the fish of the sea and the birds of the air and over every living creature that moves on the ground"* (Genesis 1:26-28).

These simple statements are the basis upon which your divine potential rests. These are the words that the Creator of the universe, who spoke it into existence, spoke over humanity. These words are powerful! They have great implications! Let us look at them individually and personalize them.

The Word of Your Endless Empowerment
Word #1 – You were created by God in His image and likeness.
Word #2 – You were blessed by God.

The Word of Your Divine Directives
Word #3 – You were commanded by God to be fruitful.
Word #4 – You were commanded by God to multiply.
Word #5 – You were commanded by God to replenish the earth.
Word #6 – You were commanded by God to subdue the earth.
Word #7 – You were commanded by God to have dominion over the earth.

I remind you that it is a spiritual law that God's Word does not change. Whatever He has commanded will stand forever. The sun still shines; the heavens still exist; birds still fly; fish still swim. All that He spoke over the man also still stands to this day. At the same time, the choice He gave man to go his own way (with consequences) also still remains.

Because of the redemptive work of Christ, if we make the choice to submit to God's authority and believe His Word, we have at our disposal His power to work on our behalf. We are restored to our original position with God.

Let's look more closely at each of these words of God that reveal His purpose for our lives.

The Word of Your Endless Empowerment

Word # 1—*You Were Created by God in His Image and Likeness*

In Genesis 1:26 the Lord explains His intention for us: To be in His image and likeness. This is God's perfect will for us. He wants us to be in His image and to be like Him. It is His desire for the world to see Him in us and for us to be like Him. Look at what He says in this scripture:

> *Consecrate yourselves and be holy, because I am the Lord your God. Keep my decrees and follow them. I am the Lord, who makes you holy* (Leviticus 20:7-8).

See, it is His will for us to be like Him. Further, we learn from this that He will bring these things to pass. We have to accept the work that He is willing to do in us.

As you study God's creation in Genesis 1, you see that everything happened just as God said it would. When He said it, it came to pass without hesitation. This is one of the most powerful principles we need to understand. When God speaks a thing, it is certain to happen. Therefore, if you line up with and agree with what God says about you, it will come to pass. And no one—not even the devil—can stop it from happening, because God commanded it. You must learn to accept what God says about you. His spoken Word settles the matter.

Now, let's set the record straight with regard to God's use of the word, *man*. God is referring to both genders when He makes His pronouncements about mankind. At the beginning, He had not separated the woman from the man. His commands, therefore, apply to both males and females. When He says, "Let us make man in our image," this refers to the female also. God created both genders to be equal, to have equal access to the power and presence of Him. Therefore, if you are woman, do not allow anyone to hinder you because of your gender. God gave His divine potential to both males and females.

Regardless of what anyone thinks or says, God said that you were created in His image and likeness. Therefore, you have the God-given ability to be like Him. He will assist you in becoming more like Him every day and even to have a mind like His and the ability to do things as He would do them. Look at these confirmations:

> *Let this mind be in you, which was also in Christ Jesus* (Philippians 2:5, KJV).

> *I tell you the truth, anyone who has faith in me will do what I have been doing. He will do even greater things than these, because I am going to the Father* (John 14:12).

A king can be a king and not walk in his authority. If he doesn't acknowledge or if he doesn't know he has servants or owns a castle, he might walk the streets as a common man. He might live his entire life in a manner that is unbefitting for a king. Even though he isn't walking in his rightful position, he's still a king. When he acknowledges or becomes aware of his rightful position, he has the legal right to assume his position and authority.

You, too, may not have acknowledged or been aware of who you truly are, but because God has said you are in His image and likeness, you have the authority and power that is granted to you by His Word. God said you were created in His image and likeness, and He is the King of kings and Lord of lords. Of what kings do you think He speaks? Of what lords? He is speaking of you! His Word has said of you, *"But you are a chosen people, a royal priesthood, a holy nation, a people belonging to God, that you may declare the praises of him who called you out of darkness into his wonderful light"* (1 Peter 2:9).

The world does not want you to be aware of your royalty. Never listen to the world; instead, always listen to what God says in His Word. You must get it into your mind that the God who spoke the universe into existence also has spoken over you. The only reason His Word cannot manifest in your life, as He has spoken it, is that you have not fully accepted the reality of its power and who you are.

You must remember at all times, GOD SAID YOU WERE CREATED IN HIS IMAGE AND HIS LIKENESS. It doesn't matter what the world tries to tell you or convince you of, or the circumstances you may find yourself in. God's powerful and endless Word has empowered you as a creation in His image and likeness.

When you wake up to the fact that you're royalty, you will alter your behavior and act differently. You will begin to walk in your rightful position in accordance with the authority that your Lord and King gives to you. You must choose to be the person God calls you to be. Your choice is powerful! Remember, God honored the choice of Adam and Eve, even to the extent that it resulted in the suffering of all mankind. How much more will He honor your choice to truly live in His image and likeness?

In being created in His image and likeness, we contain the presence of Almighty God within us. His presence gives us the ability to triumph over all things in life. He has said that He will never leave us nor forsake us. There is no place where we can go that God will not be present with us in our time of need. He is forever with us. We have but to fellowship and commune with Him and allow Him to work through us to give us the joys and the rewards of life that we desire. The presence of God gives us victory. Even in the midst of insurmountable obstacles, His presence gives power for our lives to be improved.

Consider, now, the force of His presence in this biblical example:

> *The Lord was with Joseph and he prospered, and he lived in the house of his Egyptian master. When his master saw that the Lord was with him and that the Lord gave him success in everything he did, Joseph found favor in his eyes and became his attendant. Potiphar put him in charge of his household, and he entrusted to his care everything he owned. From the time he put him in charge of his household and of all that he owned, the Lord blessed the household of the Egyptian because of Joseph. The blessing of the Lord was on everything Potiphar had, both in the house and in the field* (Genesis 39:2-5).

Here we see the young man Joseph, a slave, who prospered because of the presence of the Lord. Think of it—a rich slave! Whoever heard of such a thing? But we see it clearly; the presence of the Lord caused a slave to prosper. Not only that, but God's presence was so obviously with him that his master put him in charge of his entire household. Then, as a result of the presence of God in Joseph the slave, even the slave-master prospered. Such a tremendous power is available to us all when we recognize that we are created in the image of God and have God's power within us.

By considering some of the attributes of God, and recognizing the first word of your endless empowerment, you learn more of your awesome divine potential.

Think now ...
- Does God fail?
- Is God broke?
- Is God depressed?
- Is He struggling to get by?
- Does He want to give up on life?
- Is God afraid of tomorrow?
- Does God consider himself to be a failure?

You can boldly say no to all of the above. Now, if someone had to answer the same questions concerning you, would they be able to boldly say no? If they can't, don't be discouraged because you can change what you have been. <u>You have a divine potential given to you by God to do all things through Christ who strengthens you.</u> (See Philippians 4:13.)

When you choose to walk in and reflect God's image on earth, His power flows through you. Read what Paul wrote:

> *But now you must rid yourselves of all such things as these: anger, rage, malice, slander, and filthy language from your lips. Do not lie to each other, since you have taken off your old self with its practices and have put on the new self, which is being renewed in knowledge in the image of its Creator. Here there is no Greek or Jew, circumcised or uncircumcised, barbarian, Scythian, slave or free, but Christ is all, and is in all. Therefore, as God's chosen people, holy and dearly loved, clothe yourselves with compassion, kindness, humility, gentleness and patience (Colossians 3:8-12).*

This great teacher tells you that as you rid yourself of those things that are in no way in or of God and learn the truth, you will reflect the true image of our Creator. The world doesn't teach you this. On the contrary, it tries to keep you from recognizing it. In fact, you probably accept that there are certain things you cannot change about your life. When you accept the negative and believe that you can do nothing about it, you are also accepting the principle that you cannot be as God wants you to be.

The devil wants you to look to what the world says as being important, but God looks at you as one who was created in His image and likeness and as one who has been restored to His image and likeness through His Son, Jesus. You are His child. You are not of this world. You are not bound by its rules and regulations. You are an ambassador for the Kingdom of Heaven, and you have diplomatic immunity. You have the right to walk as a child of the King.

Consider yourself in the image and likeness of God. Stop letting the world try to put you in a category that is limited by your race, your economic status, your education, your occupation, or any other categorization that the world may use to hinder your ability to be of great benefit to mankind. Recognize who you are; declare and hold on to what God has said about you, regardless of your worldly circumstances. The Word of God will work mightily in you and accomplish what you have faith for God to do in you. The Word of God cannot be stopped. Proclaim yourself to be a child of God, who was created to be more and more like Him each and every day!

God's will for your life is certain to come to pass when you agree with it and walk in the knowledge of it. But you must remember that it is progressive. He will move you from one level to a higher level when you prove yourself faithful at the level where you are. He never moves you downward. You will simply remain where you are until you are ready for the next level. This growth is part of a one-day-at-a-time process—it is not a one-time event. It will take time, but it is certain to occur when you set yourself in agreement with what God has said about you. Nothing can stop you!

God wouldn't give you a commission to live your life in His image and likeness if He didn't give you the potential to accomplish it. He has stated;

> *Be imitators of God, therefore, as dearly loved children* (Ephesians 5:1).

Considering this, you already have the ability. Walk in it!

Remember, God gave you endless empowerment by creating you in His image and likeness. Your divine potential, which was lost by Adam, has been recovered and offered back to you through the life and death of Jesus Christ. Therefore, recognize this one more subtle but essential point: the image is more complete in you because Jesus is in you.

Act now—time is precious, so:

- Stop making excuses.
- Refuse to listen to the world's attempts to limit your abilities.
- Hear and obey the Word of God.

- See yourself as a reflection of God on the earth and live like it.
- He gives you the ability to do it.
- Believe what He has said about you.
- Because you were created in God's image, you have been given endless empowerment.
- Now, *WALK IN IT!*

Word # 2—*God's Continual Blessing*

In Genesis 1:28 we read: *"God blessed them."* The word *bless* means "to impart by spoken word goodness, favor, and good things upon others." This includes physical things as well as spiritual things. Such things include health, prosperity, vitality, favor, happiness, well-being, comfort, security, and protection. When a person blesses another, it shows willingness to impart goodness and favor to him or her. Thus, when God blessed Adam and Eve, He was empowering them by His all-powerful Word with the potential to receive good things beyond their comprehension and to cause such good things to manifest in their lives by His power.

We live in a blessed state that brings glory to God by the good things that occur in our lives. In Luke 12:32, we read the words of Jesus: *"Do not be afraid, little flock, for your Father has been pleased to give you the kingdom."*

There is further confirmation of His will in this matter, as we see in the following verses:

> *Praise be to the God and Father of our Lord Jesus Christ, who has blessed us in the heavenly realms with every spiritual blessing in Christ* (Ephesians 1:3).

> *For the Lord God is a sun and shield; the Lord bestows favor and honor; no good thing does he withhold from those whose walk is blameless* (Psalm 84:11).

> *For surely, O Lord, you bless the righteous; you surround them with your favor as with a shield* (Psalm 5:12).

The will of God to bless His children has never been and never will be revoked. God is so serious about doing good things for us that He sent His Son so that we might truly lay hold of the good things He has in store for us.

> *He who did not spare his own Son, but gave him up for us all—how will he not also, along with him, graciously give us all things?* (Roman 8:32)

What God blesses remains blessed. When God blesses you, no one can curse you. Nothing negative has authority to overcome you. Oh, yes, you may have setbacks, but you have the ability to subdue and take dominion over all the earth and anything life throws at you. God has empowered you and guaranteed you success because of His blessing. Seize it!

The ancient world understood the power of being blessed by God. You may be familiar with the story of Jacob wrestling with an angel. (See Genesis 32:22-32.) What was the reason for this wrestling match? It is clear when we study the Scripture and realize Jacob wrestled with the angel and refused to let him go until he blessed him. Jacob was willing to wrestle with an angel because he recognized the importance of being blessed.

Our problem today is that we don't realize the power that is associated with being blessed by God. Once we truly begin to understand that being blessed by God brings with it more than we could ever hope for or imagine, we should pursue our divine potential vigorously. We must wrestle with those things in life that prevent us from having a closer relationship with the Almighty God, because it is from that relationship that all our blessings flow.

When people, thoughts, or circumstances seem to work against you, you do not have to be overwhelmed by them. Remember you were endlessly empowered by God to experience good things in your life when He blessed Adam and Eve. Within you lies the ability to change every negative circumstance you encounter because of this blessing.

Adam and Eve had the ability to remain in the perfect blessings of God, but the serpent robbed them of this blessed state with his seductive, persuasive words. The enemy is still alive in the earth today. His mission is to steal, kill, destroy, and prevent God's children from experiencing the fullness of God's blessing. The scripture says he prowls around like a lion, seeking to find someone he can devour. (See 1 Peter 5:8.) He is still seeking to rob you of your blessings. However, he cannot get to everybody. He is only successful with those who do not understand who they truly are in Christ Jesus.

The divine potential to defeat satan resides within you through the power of Christ within you. This power is released when you submit to Christ as your Lord. Then, when you allow the power of Christ within you to be manifest, satan will flee from you. He has already been defeated by Christ at Calvary and is very much afraid of Him in you and working through you.

Therefore, stand on the authority of God's Word, knowing that He has blessed you! Don't be afraid of the devil's roar. Exercise the divine potential in you and defeat him. Because you have been blessed, you can maintain your confidence in every endeavor you undertake in your life. You can face life with bold courage. You know that no matter what happens, you have been blessed in all things, and all things will work together for your good. (See Romans 8:28.) There is nothing that can happen to you that God will not work out for your good. You can say with confidence, "I am blessed by God, and nothing in the universe can take His blessings away from me."

There is no way to define the fullness of God's blessings upon us, because He " ... *is able to do immeasurably more than all we ask or imagine, according to his power that is at work within us*" (Ephesians 3:20). Your knowledge of God's continual blessings expands exponentially as you read them throughout the scriptures. I list only a few below, leaving a volume of additional blessings for you to discover:

- **The Holy Spirit abiding in you.** You're blessed with unlimited potential through the power of the Holy Spirit! You have the ability to be His witness " . . . *to the ends of the earth*" (Acts 1:8).

- **Fear is defeated.** The Spirit is *" … power … love, and … a sound mind"* (2 Timothy 1:7, KJV). In other words, the Spirit is power to eradicate fear.
- **You are *"blessed in heavenly realms."*** You're blessed in the *" … heavenly realms with every spiritual blessing in Christ"* (Ephesians 1:3). This is the divine potential that reaches into the spiritual world and achieves supernatural results in the natural.
- **You have the power to bless others.** You're blessed with the divine potential to bless others and glorify God. (See James 3:8-13 and Romans 15:6.)
- **Above all, God has blessed you with His Word.** "His Word" includes His exceedingly great promises. Through them, you partake of His divine nature and escape the world's decay. (See 2 Peter 1:4.)

There are so many Scriptures that pertain to your being blessed in countless ways, and each of these releases your ability to move beyond your natural circumstances and environment into His greatness. You have the ability to do it! God promised this through His Word. And He never makes a promise without following through on it.

God said it; therefore, it's true that you have been *blessed* with five divine directives that God is obligated to assist you in accomplishing:

- Be fruitful.
- Multiply.
- Replenish the earth.
- Subdue.
- Take dominion.

All subsequent blessings flow from these divine directives. Everything you need comes from these and the Word of endless empowerment that God has spoken over you. You have a divine right for these blessings to manifest in your life right now.

As we continue our study, you will find that *you* are the greatest hindrance to God's power working on your behalf in your life. You alone determine how much of your divine potential will manifest in your life. God has given you freedom of choice. Now choose to continue to pursue the reality of your divine potential.

We will review your divine directives in the next chapter, but as for now, take a few moments to really consider what it means to be blessed by Almighty God.

CHAPTER 3

The Revelation of Your Divine Directives

God's Commands Enable Your Triumph

God blessed them and said to them, "Be fruitful and increase in number; fill the earth and subdue it. Rule over the fish of the sea and the birds of the air and over every living creature that moves on the ground" (Genesis 1:28).

This is one of the most powerful verses that was ever written in the Bible. In this single verse, God empowers mankind with five divine directives that give His people the authority and power to take control over the earth.

Although they were spoken to Adam, they apply to us, and they are an untapped source of confidence for us. In these we see God's original plan for us. And let us remember that whatever God established in the beginning is still applicable today. He does not change.

Let us now consider each of these divine directives and what they mean for us. We will see how they give us strength to know that God's command and His power support us in accomplishing those things He has called us to do. We're now going to look at the power these divine directives unleash in our lives.

The Force of the Word of God

Let's begin with the first three verses in the Bible in order to learn the force of the spoken Word of God:

In the beginning God created the heavens and the earth. Now the earth was formless and empty, darkness was over the surface of the deep, and the Spirit of God was hovering over the waters. And God said, "Let there be light," and there was light (Genesis 1:1-3).

When God created the heavens and the earth, the earth was not pleasing to God. "*Darkness was over the surface of the deep,*" so God said, "*Let there be light ... and there was light.*" In the midst of darkness, God brought the light into existence by simply commanding it to exist. An energy force that never existed came into existence simply by the spoken directive of God. Even to this day, the light He spoke into existence in the beginning of time remains, as it is with everything He created from the beginning.

We should also take note that when the scripture states, "*In the beginning God created the heaven and the earth,*" we see all things created in submission to the spoken Word of Almighty God. When we speak of the "beginning," we are speaking of time. When we speak of "the heavens," we are speaking of space. When we speak of "the earth," we are speaking of matter. These three entities are totally responsive, without challenge, to any directives God gives. The meaning of this is simple: there is nothing in existence in our universe that will not respond to a directive from God. Whatever He commands of time, space, or matter will respond immediately and obediently because it all exists for His pleasure.

All things in the universe, with the exception of man, were created without having the freedom of choice. Therefore, whatever God commanded or commands is done even if it violates laws we consider impossible to violate—no ifs, ands, or buts. Man, on the other hand, was created with the freedom of choice and a free will. Because God gave him a free will, man has always had the option to either agree with God's divine commands or challenge them.

Our challenges to what God commands seriously diminish the quality of life we experience. God created everything with a purpose and a plan. When we submit to God's commands, the presence of God in us causes the universe to get in line with His will to allow us to accomplish what He has commanded. There is no force in the universe that will not ultimately submit to the directives of God. This is one of the most exciting revelations for us. Being created in the image of God means we have been designed to contain the presence and power of God within us. Armed with this knowledge, if we are seeking to do anything according to His will, we can truly say, *"If God is for us, who can be against us?"* (Romans 8:31). Then we can also say, *"No weapon formed against us shall prosper."* (See Isaiah 54:17.)

When we see what God says about us, we will know we have the power to live rich and rewarding lives. Now, let's review the divine directives that were given to man in this powerful scripture.

Divine Directive #1—Be Fruitful/Productive!

God said, *"Be fruitful."* This means He wants us to be productive, not just to have many children. It means to be productive at whatever you set your hand to do—far exceeding anything you have ever imagined.

Consider what it means to be fruitful. God had already defined the word in Genesis 1:11-12: *"Then God said, 'Let the land produce vegetation: seed-bearing plants and trees on the land that **bear fruit with seed in it**, according to their various kinds.' And it was so. The land produced vegetation: plants bearing seed according to their kinds and trees bearing **fruit with seed in it** according to their kinds. And God saw that it was good"*(emphasis mine).

Notice the use of the word *fruit*. God is the first to use this word. Both times the word *fruit* is mentioned, we see that fruit has a unique characteristic. It has seed in it!

A seed has the ability to produce more fruit. Consider one apple. We can count the number of seeds in the apple. But can you tell me this? How many apples will come from each seed? Each seed has the potential to produce an apple tree, and each tree has any number of seasons during which it may produce multiple apples. The potential vast number of apples that may come from a single seed is incalculable.

What does this mean for us? God commanded us not only to produce fruit but to invoke a chain reaction. He has commanded us to produce fruit that contains seed that produces more fruit that contains seed that produces much more fruit.

God's divine directive to us is not just to produce fruit, but to be *fruitful*, which means that we are to be full of fruit that contains multiple seeds that produce a tremendous quantity of fruit. God has created us for greatness!

Now, if we use the word productive, we realize that God intends for us to be productive beyond measure. And that productivity has within it the seed to produce more productivity. God desires for a man or woman to be abundantly productive in his or her life, exceeding the capacity of people to even consider it. And that productivity in a person's life is to overflow to their children and their grandchildren and their great, grandchildren. This productivity is so great that it is not limited to a person's family and generations, but it exceeds the boundaries of the person's family to be beneficial to the society in which he or she lives. It is God's desire for you to be so productive and have such an overwhelming abundance that you will have much to share with the community in which you live. It is possible for a truly fruitful individual to leave a lasting legacy for multiple generations and nations in the future. Indeed, God's Word to you is: "*I will bless you, and you will be a blessing.*" (See Genesis 12:2.)

God has authorized this type of productivity for you. In fact, He has given you a divine directive for you to experience it and be a blessing to your family and your generation.

Knowing this, there is no need for you to settle for anything less than success in life. God has commanded you to be fruitful in whatever He gives you to do. It doesn't matter whether you are in school or on the job, you possess the ability to excel in whatever you undertake.

You can be the top student, the top sales producer, the best employee. This is all because God has commanded you to be productive. When you set yourself in agreement with His command, God will work in you to assist you in accomplishing what He has commanded. Furthermore, He will command His angels to assist you in being successful. God, His universe, and everything He created in it work together to propel you toward a life of extreme fruitfulness and productivity. You have the seed of productivity in you. Allow it to take root and begin to produce fruit.

In John 15:2 Jesus said that every branch in Him would bear fruit. Then He said that the branches would be pruned so that they would bear even more fruit. There will come times in your life when you will be pruned by God to be even more productive. You may not recognize these times as times of pruning. You may see them as stumbling blocks that have been thrown in your way. You may even feel that you cannot overcome them. But, I want you to remember this: When God is in you, stumbling blocks are merely steppingstones to higher levels in life.

Now you may be one of those who has thought of yourself as "nothing," as someone who is unable to accomplish any great thing in your entire life, but I want to assure you that God has given you a divine directive to be fruitful. You are going to come into the realization of your divine potential as you yield your will to God. Then, He will transform your "nothing" into something that is useable, incredible, and reproducible.

A little boy went to a religious camp meeting. His mother packed a lunch for him so that he would have something to eat. He heard a minister speak to a large crowd of people that had gathered there. After a period of time, he heard the minister ask members of his staff, "Where can we find food for these people to eat?" His staff informed him that they did not have enough money to feed the large crowd. One of his assistants recognized the boy with his lunch and commented, *"Here is a boy with five loaves and two small fish, but what is this lunch among so many?" The minister took the boy's food, blessed it, and then had his assistants give it to those who were there. Every man, woman, and child had as much as they wanted to eat. Then the minister said, "Gather the pieces that are left over. Let nothing be wasted."* When they gathered all of the pieces that were left, there were still twelve baskets of leftovers!

Now, do I have to tell you who this minister was? Jesus took this little something, which was considered nothing, and fed more than 5,000 people with it! (See John 6:5-13.) God will take the little you have and do exceedingly great things with it when you believe.

Now confess these things over your life:
- I am somebody, even when it appears as though I have nothing. I have more than meets the eye.
- I have a creative and productive mind. I develop solutions for problems when others cannot.
- My willingness to allow God to use me means that His power works in me for my success in life.
- I can do all things through Christ who strengthens me!

Please do not mistake these confessions as being mere words; remember what God did with words. You are created in His image and likeness, and you have the ability to be fruitful, even though you might not have recognized it until right now. You're expected to yield good fruit in everything you do. The irony is that a fulfilled and blessed life in Christ originates from fruit-bearing. When you produce with the little you have, you're given even more. (See Matthew 25:21, 29.) In other words, as you obey God, you're blessed with even more fruit. Below are some scriptures that pertain to your productivity:

- **Hear His Word.** The Parable of the Sower: *"The one who received the seed that fell on good soil is the man who hears the word and understands it. He produces a crop, yielding a hundred, sixty or thirty times what was sown"* (Matthew 13:23).

- **Obey and prosper.** *"If they obey and serve him, they will spend the rest of their days in prosperity and their years in contentment"* (Job 36:11).

- **Delight in God's Word and bear fruit.** *"Blessed is the man who does not walk in the counsel of the wicked or stand in the way of sinners or sit in the seat of mockers. But his delight is in the law of the LORD, and on his law he meditates day and night. He is like a tree planted by streams of water, which yields its fruit in season and whose leaf does not wither. Whatever he does prospers"* (Psalm 1:1-3).

- **Be strong and courageous; then nothing and no one will be able to stand against you.** *"No one will be able to stand up against you all the days of your life. As I was with Moses, so I will be with you; I will never leave you nor forsake you. Be strong and courageous, because you will lead these people to inherit the land I swore to their forefathers to give them. Be strong and very courageous. Be careful to obey all the law my servant Moses gave you; do not turn from it to the right or to the left, that you may be successful wherever you go. Do not let this Book of the Law depart from your mouth; meditate on it day and night, so that you may be careful to do everything written in it. Then you will be prosperous and successful. Have I not commanded you? Be strong and courageous. Do not be terrified; do not be discouraged, for the LORD your God will be with you wherever you go"* (Joshua 1:5-9).

God has given you so many great and precious promises concerning your life. Therefore, avoid unproductive, negative words, thoughts, and actions that violate the Word of God. They will rob you of your productivity. Also, as it is stated in Psalm 1, separate yourself from those who have a negative influence on your life. Rather, focus on what God says.

Decide today that you will make every effort to understand and speak the Word of God with regard to your life. Meditate and delight in it because His Word is your life. As He has stated in Deuteronomy 32:47, His words are not idle. By them, you will live long. So, stay close and serve God through obedience to what His Word says about you. You will be transformed into His image, and you will develop strength and courage to fulfill the mission He has set apart for you.

Now, meditate on these biblical truths as a child of God:
- God has given you the blessing to be fruitful.

- You can produce something out of small things (sometimes called "nothing")—yielding thirty, sixty or a hundred times more than you sow.
- You're productive and successful in whatever endeavors you undertake.
- You're prosperous and successful wherever you go.
- The end result of your obedience is increased productivity for greater success.

Divine Directive #2—Multiply in Number!

God said, "*Increase [multiply] in number.*" Because God has empowered you, you will yield fruit. God desires your fruitful life to multiply and reflect His image to others in the world, thus making the world better—just as He did in the beginning.

Frequently the word "multiply" is interpreted to mean, "to reproduce and have more children." But there is no glory for God in the world being populated with men and women who rebel against Him. God is not only talking about multiplying people in the earth. In this verse He is giving Adam a divine directive to multiply people in His image in the earth.

You're not to just reproduce yourself; you are to multiply the image of God on earth by causing other people to recognize the qualities of God in them. And then they themselves are to "multiply"—to cause others to become more godly.

God created man in His image to be a reflection of himself in the earth. In a sense, therefore, God was reproducing himself. But, as a result of the free will that was given to him, man decided that he wanted to be like God. He chose not to be a reflection of God in the earth, but he wanted to be as a god himself. This greatly displeased God. As a result, man fell from the lofty estate that God had originally designed for him and has lived an inferior life-style ever since. The original intention of God was for His people to be a reflection of Him, fulfilling His divine potential and submitting to His will. So when God said, "Multiply," He meant that man was to multiply His image throughout the earth. The only way to accomplish this is for a person to accept Jesus as his or her Lord and Savior and become a true reflection of the image of God as it is revealed in Christ.

This is the key to your prosperity. As you submit to His will and multiply His image on earth, God increases your natural blessings so you can glorify Him even more. You multiply His image and presence by causing more and more people to turn to Him and become like Him. Think! Wouldn't this world be much better if more people were like Christ?

When you have submitted yourself to God, there are many ways to multiply His image:

- **You multiply His image by giving of yourself.** Remember that God is a Giver, and He gives to you. When you give, you reflect Him and demonstrate His presence that is within you.

- **You multiply His image when you actively serve in a ministry to support the gospel.** In the early Church, some men were chosen to be deacons while others served, labored, and helped in other capacities. Serving in ministry is as important now as it was then.

  And the Word of God increased; and the number of the disciples multiplied in Jerusalem greatly; and a great company of the priests were obedient to the faith (Acts 6:7, KJV).

- **You multiply His image when you promote the ministry through financial contributions.** As you read the following, realize that when they *"sent him* [Paul] *forth,"* finances were most certainly used. Make a mental note of how the Church "multiplied" as a result of this:

  *... and sent him forth to Tarsus. Then had the churches rest throughout all Judaea and Galilee and Samaria, and were edified; and walking in the fear of the Lord, and in the comfort of the Holy Ghost, were **multiplied*** (Acts 9:30-31, KJV, emphasis mine).

- **You multiply His image when God gives back to you. This will make you more fruitful and will multiply His image even further.** God wants to do more than just increase your finances. He wants to multiply them so that you will be generous on every occasion. (See 2 Corinthians 9:11.)

Remember this: Whoever sows sparingly will also reap sparingly, and whoever sows generously will also reap generously. Each man should give what he has decided in his heart to give, not reluctantly or under compulsion, for God loves a cheerful giver. And God is able to make all grace abound to you, so that in all things at all times, having all that you need, you will abound in every good work (2 Corinthians 9:6-8).

- **You multiply His image when you do your part to assist in the spreading of the gospel throughout the world.** God increases your harvest so you can spread the gospel to others. Do you recall Elijah and the widow in 1 Kings 17:14-18? During a famine, God commanded Elijah to go to a widow who was not an Israelite and ask her to supply food for him. See how her giving the little she had was returned greatly:

For this is what the Lord, the God of Israel, says: 'The jar of flour will not be used up and the jug of oil will not run dry until the day the Lord gives rain on the land.' She went away and did as Elijah had told her. So there was food every day for Elijah and for the woman and her family. For the jar of flour was not used up and the jug of oil did not run dry, in keeping with the word of the Lord spoken by Elijah (1 Kings 14-18).

As this woman became a part of the work of the Prophet Elijah, God blessed her family. Even though it was during a time of famine, her household had abundance. Again, this is a very important point for you to remember: as you partner with God, God increases your blessings so that you might be more of a blessing to others. All that He gives to you is not for you. A part of it is for the work of the Kingdom in reproducing His image in the earth.

You have many ways to exercise this potential. God is looking for men and women just like you, who are willing to let Him work in their lives. He's looking for you. He " ... *wants all men to be saved and to come to a knowledge of the truth*" (1 Timothy 2:4). When you commit yourself to assisting Him in this endeavor, God partners with you and assists you in achieving your divine potential. It is His pleasure to increase your productivity for His glory.

Now recognize that your divine potential is within your grasp when you commit yourself to multiplying God's image and likeness on the face of the earth.

Divine Directive #3—Replenish the Earth

In Genesis 1:28, God gave a directive to Adam and Eve: *"Fill* [replenish] *the earth."* He was telling them to continue His work and replenish or *make complete* the earth. They were to fill up the earth with His image and likeness and add value to it. To fill up something that is empty, you must have something with which to fill it. Adam and Eve had the blessing of the presence of the Almighty God within them. Just like God, they were to improve the state of the things with which they came into contact. In this case, it was the earth and all that was in it.

Do you understand that God has given you the potential to add value to the earth? He has given you His blessing to make it a better place—a much better place. You are just beginning to recognize the awesome, still-untapped potential in you. Your life and creative abilities are worth more than all the gold of the world. This creative potential allows you to look at a situation and determine solutions that even the most gifted, learned people cannot. You have the ability to tap into the divine Creator of all things and create solutions that have never before been realized. God considers you more valuable than a thousand universes, and you are worth the greatest of all sacrifices to Him. For this reason, God sent His only Son into the world to give His life so that you might be reconciled unto Him.

Your life is precious to Him because He knows the potential that is within you. He knows because He put it there.

He created heaven and the earth just for you, and He gave you the divine directive to make this world complete and finish His work. Because God is the Creator and builder of all universes, the same potential is within you to create and build a better society for generations to come. You were created with the ability not to just see things as they are, but to see things as they can be. You can improve upon things that already exist. You're able to take on projects and leave things in better condition than they were before you got involved. You don't leave things half-done or unfinished. You prosper in whatever you set your hand to do. You're able to make things complete. The creative talent within you that was given to you by God through His divine directives has empowered you with this potential.

Keep this in mind: the potential within you is divine. It is not your ability, it is His.

> *Now unto him that is able to do exceeding abundantly above all that we ask or think, according to the power that worketh in us* (Ephesians 3:20, KJV).

It is your honor, therefore, to allow God to work in you and through you. He is always there to assist you in accomplishing His will. Your divine directive is to fill the earth, to make it complete, and to add value to everything you encounter. The creative genius is within you. Accept it with boldness!

Divine Directive #4—Subdue *IT*

God knew from the beginning that your ability to be valuable and prosperous would be challenged, so He gave you power to defeat those challenges before you even encountered them.

God said, *"Subdue it"* (Genesis 1:28).

Subdue means "to dominate, force, or keep under." It means that you're able to overcome all of the obstinate obstacles of the world that stand in your way. Nothing can defeat you. Absolutely nothing!

But what specifically are you supposed to subdue and overcome? Now think for a moment as we consider this statement: God said to subdue *it*. Broadly, this means that you have the authority to subdue anything that comes against you on earth. *It* can mean anything: sickness, fear, problems, negative thoughts, poverty—anything that is not of God. No matter what *it* is, you have the ability to subdue *it*!

Consider these scriptures so you will be able to clearly understand that God wants you to subdue anything contrary to His will on earth:

> *But thanks be to God, who always leads us in triumphal procession in Christ and through us spreads everywhere the fragrance of the knowledge of him* (2 Corinthians 2:14).

> *And these signs will accompany those who believe: In my name they will drive out demons; they will speak in new tongues; they will pick up snakes with their hands; and when they drink deadly poison, it will not hurt them at all; they will place their hands on sick people, and they will get well* (Mark 16:17-18).

> *I have given you authority to trample on snakes and scorpions and to overcome all the power of the enemy; nothing will harm you* (Luke 10:19).

Wake up! God will not let *it* come on you more than what you are able to handle. (See 1 Corinthians 10:13). You have the divine potential and the power to subdue *it* and vanquish any foe. Nothing and no one can keep you down. You have been created with a divine directive to be more than a conqueror. You are destined to be an overcomer. He has given you a divine directive to subdue any force. God gives you the ability to subdue anything that will ever exist in time, space, or matter, including:

- the devil and all enemies
- worldly views
- personal weaknesses

- mountains of life
- weapons that are formed against you
- sickness and disease
- undesirable circumstances
- inner conflicts
- financial lack and debt
- drugs or alcohol
- addictions

God would never give you a directive to subdue a thing if He did not give you the ability to do it. Always keep this in mind: the challenges you face in life have no ability to overcome you or stop you from accomplishing the mission God has called you to accomplish in life. Stand and face the issue. Don't be afraid of the enemy that is before you. Recognize that God knew this day would come and He has already equipped you with the ability to triumph.

Don't spend your time cursing the enemy or anything that is against you. Rather, focus your energies on allowing the force within you to confront your adversary. The challenges you face have not taken God off guard. Jesus told us that in this world we would have trouble, but He also said that we were not to worry because He has overcome the world. (See John 16:33.) Therefore, allow His presence, power, and force to deal with every adversary you face.

The circumstances of your life have come to strengthen you. In addition, with each and every trial you face, the force of the power of God within you is strengthened, and this will allow you to grow from one glorious triumph to another. As the Word of God has said, you will go from glory to glory.

Consider carefully what God says below:

> *No temptation has seized you except what is common to man. And God is faithful; he will not let you be tempted beyond what you can bear. But when you are tempted, he will also provide a way out so that you can stand up under it* (1 Corinthians 10:13).

This scripture has been quoted many times to offer comfort to those who need to remember that God does not allow us to be tempted beyond what we can bear. But I want to emphasize a phrase that I think is much more important. He states, " ... *he will also provide a way out.*" Do you see this?

God is saying that He will provide a way out! Many of us feel we must continue to accept and endure negative situations as a way of life. We think that it must be God's will for us to suffer in the trials we face. But I appeal to you to recognize that Jesus came so you might have life abundantly and that God has provided a way out for you. Therefore, seek His way out, for God receives more glory in your *subduing* the enemy than in your *enduring* the enemy.

The scripture says that He has provided a way out, but that way may not be immediately apparent to you. Don't let this discourage you, however, because it is God's way. He has said:

> *It is the glory of God to conceal a matter; to search out a matter is the glory of kings* (Proverbs 25:2).

The solution to your problem and your ability to subdue it have already been made available to you. All you have to do is to seek them out. God says that it is to the glory of kings to search out a matter that He has concealed. Think about this: all major advancements that have ever been made by mankind required someone taking the time to evaluate the problem. Then, by the creative force within them, they discovered the solution that enabled them to overcome the problem. Every challenge that mankind has ever faced has been overcome through diligent effort and a faithful commitment of time. God desires for you to turn to Him to determine the appropriate action that is necessary to subdue your adversary.

God has given you His Holy Spirit to communicate with in order to determine the action you need to take. Though it is hidden from you for the moment, it will be given to you at the right time. Jesus said:

For whatever is hidden is meant to be disclosed, and whatever is concealed is meant to be brought out into the open (Mark 4:22).

This is God's promise. Every problem or issue you encounter in life has a solution. It is merely a matter of time before you discover it. Don't give up hope; keep on pursuing your goal relentlessly. For all you know, the next thought you have may be the one that reveals to you how to subdue that one issue or problem that has been confronting you.

Since the time when God ended the creation process, nothing new under the sun has been created. The answers to all problems have already been created. They are simply waiting to be discovered. If there is an issue that has confronted you, take heart; God has equipped you with the ability to discover the solution that will enable you to subdue it. Remember that you have a divine directive to subdue the earth and everything that is in it. This is a part of your divine potential.

Everything that has been created by God and exists in time, space, or matter has the ability to be subdued by people. No matter what it is, whether gravity, the laws of physics, or other universal laws, they have all been able to be used by people in order for them to accomplish His purposes. When people partner with God; the impossible is accomplished.

The laws of the universe were completely obliterated by the warrior Joshua when he told the sun to stand still so that he might fulfill the purposes of God, and, indeed, the sun stood still. (See Joshua 10:12-13.) If we consider the reality of this taking place, as the Bible said it did, this means that the earth had to stop spinning on its axis. The whole universe ceased its motion, and the sun stood still because a man had commanded it to do so. Joshua allowed himself to fulfill the divine potential that God placed within him.

Three young Hebrew men—Shadrach, Meshach, and Abednego— defied not only the great King Nebuchadnezzar but also the physical laws of fire. When they were thrown into the fiery furnace, the flames did not harm them. (See Daniel 3.)

What great work has God called you to do?

There is no limitation to your ability when you allow God to work through you. Because of your divine directive to subdue, the difference between the possible and the impossible in your life is only a matter of time. The possible you will deal with immediately, but the impossible might take you a little while. There are many things in the history of mankind that were considered impossible, but in the course of time they were proven possible. Therefore, you must not allow your lack of knowledge of God's solution to prevent you from recognizing that there is no challenge that you cannot subdue.

Many things that we encounter are indeed impossible or cause us unnecessary hardship because of the approach we take to achieve them. We may waste time and expend enormous amounts of effort in attempting to climb the mountain that appears to block our path on our way to achieving some goal. Perhaps in actuality, all we had to do was speak to the mountain and tell it to be removed, and it would have been cast into the sea.

Things that are impossible in one way are often possible in another. As the old saying goes: "There's more than one way to skin a cat." As you walk in your divine potential, God, the omniscient Master of the universe, will reveal the correct action you need to take so that you will succeed in everything you undertake, and no weapon formed against you shall prosper.

Remember, I have been encouraging you all along to recognize your partnership with God. The power of your divine potential being manifested in your life is directly related to your ability to accept the authority and Lordship of God in your life. Now:

> *Submit yourselves therefore to God. Resist the devil [or the mountain you face], and he will flee from you* (James 4:7).

Keep this in mind: to subdue *it* requires **action** on your part. Stop submitting to things that have no right to subdue you. God has given you the ability to subdue *it*, so exercise your ability to do so by submitting to God, and then confront the *it* your life and subdue *it*. Put forth the effort to challenge those things that you know are contrary to the will of God. Your victory has already been assured! Go for it!

Divine Directive #5—**Have Dominion**

The fifth divine directive God gave us in Genesis 1:28 is, *"Rule"* (have dominion). God tells you to bring things into order, to rule, manage, discipline, and control those things that you have subdued. Now let's be clear about this; you not only have the right to subdue *it* (whatever *it* is), but also to rule over *it.* Subduing life's challenges is only half the battle. You also have been given the divine directive to take *full* authority over them!

God said that you are to rule over all the earth! By God's authority, you have the right to rule over everything that tries to dominate you. If poverty, sickness, the devil, or trouble challenges you, you have the right to rule over it. Nothing in the earth has the authority to set limitations upon you. You do not have to accept being dominated by anything that God has given you authority over. Stop allowing it! Recognize the divine potential in you and disregard the arbitrary limitations set by the world's voices and circumstances. You were created to take dominion over the world and its circumstances.

While it is God's intention for us to rule over all the earth, we sometimes lose sight of that. The world or the devil plants seeds of doubt, fear, and failure in our minds and sometimes it's easy to feel helpless and, worse, hopeless. Sometimes we believe we cannot make it. We just want to give up. It seems that we have to go through one thing after another, one setback after another. We feel that we've done the best we can and it's not good enough. Discouraged, we might say things like:

- "I can't."
- "It's impossible."
- "There's no way out."
- "They won't let me."
- "This is all I've got."
- "It'll never work."
- "I'm all alone."
- "It's too hard."

But remember this: God sent Jesus to set things in order, to show us the way of the truth. He was sent to make us aware of our divine potential.

Remember, Jesus came that you might have life and that you might have it more abundantly. (See John 10:10.) Clearly, we understand that the life He's talking about is eternal life. It is an accepted fact that Jesus died so that we could have eternal life. But let me ask you, when do you actually obtain eternal life? Is this something you get when you die? Or, is it something you get at the time when you accept Christ as your Lord and Savior?

Many people are awaiting death so that they may obtain eternal life. But, scripture has made it plain that when you believe in Jesus as the Christ, you *have* eternal life then. Not *will have*, but *have* eternal life. Notice the present tense of the verb in these few scriptures:

> *Whoever believes in the Son has eternal life, but whoever rejects the Son will not see life, for God's wrath remains on him* (John 3:36).

> *I tell you the truth, whoever hears my word and believes him who sent me has eternal life and will not be condemned; he has crossed over from death to life* (John 5:24).

> *I tell you the truth, he who believes has everlasting life* (John 6:47).

> *Whoever eats my flesh and drinks my blood has eternal life, and I will raise him up at the last day* (John 6:54).

> *He who has the Son has life; he who does not have the Son of God does not have life* (1 John 5:12).

Each of the scriptures makes it plain that eternal life is for anyone who has accepted Christ. If we go back and review John 10:10, we see that Christ came to bring two things to us: eternal life and abundant life. Now, if He came to give us eternal life, and it is given to us now, then abundant life, likewise, is also given to us now.

Remembering the **Nazareth Negation**, we continue to negate the power of God to give us abundance in this life. We continue to doubt that God is able to give us victory and triumph over all of our adversaries and thereby negate His power to deliver us. We have to understand that in Jesus Christ, our God has given us complete and total victory. We simply accept the victory that has been gained for us. Once we accept it, we walk in it and live the life that has been designed for us. We experience it when we believe it is available to us.

In all of our actions, we must never allow satan to rob us of what Christ paid so dear a price for us. We have to learn to stand and demand that things, which stand in our way and challenge us, submit to the divine order of God and the divine directive that God has given us. We *can* overcome the world just as Christ has and we *can* experience triumph over those things that are against us. This power is available to you. You were created for it.

> *For we are God's workmanship, created in Christ Jesus to do good works, which God prepared in advance for us to do* (Ephesians 2:10).

Once again, I encourage and remind you that God is not a man who will lie to you. If He speaks a thing, it is true. It shall come to pass. Moreover, without faith to believe the Word of God, it is impossible to please Him. And if we do not please Him, He will not allow us to partner with Him to complete His work on earth. If He does not become our partner, we will not experience our divine potential because we will not have the power of God working with us and in us to complete us.

If you have accepted Christ, your divine potential that was granted by Almighty God is active in you:

- Now you can do all things through Christ who strengthens you. (See Philippians 4:13.) You can do as He asks because He gives you strength to do it. Ask Him for it!
- Christ has been given *"all authority in heaven and on earth"* (Matthew 28:18). And Christ says to *"go and make disciples of all nations"* (Matthew 28:19). You have a command to finish what He started. When you begin to fulfill that command, you have the right to subdue and take dominion over anything that stands in the way.

- *"And I will do whatever you ask in my name, so that the Son may bring glory to the Father. You may ask me for anything in my name, and I will do it"* (John 14:13-14).

Not only has God the Father given you a divine directive, but God the Son has given you the assurance that in His name, you can do all things. The potential available to you in the name of the Father, the Son, and the Holy Spirit is the incredible potential to be successful in all things to the glory of God.

Rule It or It Will Rule You!

Now be careful, if you don't exercise your authority to take dominion over the thing that you're battling, it will take dominion over you! Satan will see to that. Furthermore, it is a principle of God that if you have been given a gift from Him and do not use it, the gift will be taken away. This is what has happened to the Body of Christ in so many situations. Because we have been unaware of our divine potential, we have allowed satan to rule in situations in which he has no authority to rule.

You've got to learn to face *it* and get on top of *it*. Don't be afraid of *it*. Why should you run from a challenge when God has already told you that you have the victory over it? You may have been in the battle for a long time and feel as if you are not going to be successful. You may be weary, but in a short while, you will truly learn how to seize your divine potential. You have to understand that in this life we are at war against an adversary that is shrewd, cunning, and powerful. However, the power we have is far greater than his.

The Bible tells us, *"For we wrestle not against flesh and blood"* (Ephesians 6:12, KJV). We must discipline ourselves to develop our faith so that the power of the Spirit within us is released on our behalf to fight spirit with Spirit to assure our victory. We are at war. Satan is not your friend. He takes no prisoners and neither should you. Do not even enter into discussion with him. He is a liar and a deceiver. There is nothing to discuss with him.

If you think, "I can't do it because I'm poor or handicapped or lacking this or that," it's a lie! The master deceiver has deceived you. You've got to go beyond your thinking and realize that you are in the image and likeness of God. How can you be defeated if the power of God is within you? Let me use a cliché from a famous movie: "Let the force be with you."

You have the force of the Word of God with you at all times. You must learn to utilize His Word. It is the sword of the Spirit. Since satan and his demons are all spiritual beings, they can be defeated with the Word of God. Learn to use your sword. God intends for you to have the victory.

> *For our struggle is not against flesh and blood, but against the rulers, against the authorities, against the powers of this dark world and against the spiritual forces of evil in the heavenly realms. Therefore put on the full armor of God, so that when the day of evil comes, you may be able to stand your ground, and after you have done everything, to stand. Stand firm then, with the belt of truth buckled around your waist, with the breastplate of righteousness in place, and with your feet fitted with the readiness that comes from the gospel of peace. In addition to all this, take up the shield of faith, with which you can extinguish all the flaming arrows of the evil one. Take the helmet of salvation and the sword of the Spirit, which is the Word of God. (Ephesians 6:12-17)*

When evil things come against you, confront and subdue them, take dominion, and place them under your feet. Speak with authority: "I'm created in the image of God. I'll subdue and rule over anything contrary to His will for my life." Remember, your battle is not against flesh and blood, but against principalities and powers. (See Ephesians 6:12.) Use the Word of God to elevate your thoughts and actions to conform to His image. Then continue to speak the Word of God regardless of appearances, for the Bible tells us that it is the sword of the Spirit. The Word will keep the evil things that come against you at bay. God has given you the authority. It's up to you to use it.

Search the Word and find out what it says regarding your circumstance. Then do what it says. God will not let His Word return to Him void. He will step in and turn negative things around and they will actually become blessings in your life. His honor is at stake. Your circumstances will have to bow to Him and become subject to your ordained godly rule. Because of your divine potential, God makes everything work out for your good. He even turns things that you think are detrimental into blessings! (See Romans 8:28.)

Therefore, I say this to you: Rejoice at anything that comes *against* you—whether trial, tribulation, or testing—it is all an opportunity for you to strengthen yourself and exercise your ability to take dominion over it!

- Don't run from *it.*
- Don't ignore *it.*
- Don't think that because you have subdued *it,* you've won.
- Instead, take and maintain dominion over *it.*

Whatever you are up against will continue to attack you repeatedly until you take dominion over *it* and rule *it.* Pray and seek God's wisdom regarding *it*; pray with another person in agreement about *it,* and/or seek wise counsel. When you have heard from God, don't be afraid to take *it* by the force of God that's at work within you. Take *it* captive and keep *it* bound and suppressed under your dominion.

Let me suggest a few things to you now. God has already provided a way for you to triumph. He has written it in His scriptures. If you need help, get one of the books that list God's promises for your victory.

- Memorize scriptures that relate to your trial.
- Play them over and over in your head. If you're creative, turn them into melodies and sing them to yourself.
- Speak them out loud.
- Step away from the turmoil and give the situation or person (*it*) to God. Do not let *it* take root in your heart.
- Confront and subdue *it.*
- Take authority over *it.*

Here's what we are told:

*For though we live in the world, we do not wage war as the world does. The weapons we fight with are not the weapons of the world. On the contrary, they have divine power to demolish strongholds. We demolish arguments and every pretension that sets itself up against the knowledge of God, and we **take captive every thought** to make it obedient to Christ* (2 Corinthians 10:3-5, emphasis mine).

Defeat Your Greatest Enemy First

God has given you authority and power to take dominion over all things on earth. Your first responsibility, however, is to subdue and take dominion over the only enemy that can defeat you—YOU!

You cannot triumph over the external world until you subdue and take dominion over you! You will have to wage war against every argument within you that challenges what God has said about you.

You have been taught by the world to see yourself as inferior to what God's original plan was for you. Your years of conditioning and indoctrination will cause you to doubt what the Almighty has said about you. You will find yourself struggling against what God has said. Doubt and unbelief will be unrelenting in their challenge to influence you to believe what God says cannot be true.

It will take some time to undo the conditioning of years of misinformation, but God's Word is sure and powerful. If you continue hearing the Word of God over and over again, your thinking will become aligned with it and your mind will be renewed. Then, because of your persistent and diligent efforts, your life will be transformed by the renewing of your mind.

Your Victory Is Assured!

Even if victory seems impossible, it's already guaranteed by God. When you're submitted to the Lord, the battle is His. He's never defeated, so don't be afraid to confront *it* —whatever *it* is. God has already given you an assurance that you'll win. You'll triumph because He fights for you. It is only a matter of time before these things will come to pass because of Christ who works in you.

> *Not that we are competent in ourselves to claim anything for ourselves, but our competence comes from God. . . . We are hard pressed on every side, but not crushed; perplexed, but not in despair; persecuted, but not abandoned; struck down, but not destroyed* (2 Corinthians 3:5 and 4:8).

David understood this and you will also. You have to be confident in the power of the Lord.

> *David said to the Philistine, "You come against me with sword and spear and javelin, but I come against you in the name **of the LORD Almighty, the God of the armies of Israel, whom you have defied.** This day the LORD will hand you over to me, and I'll strike you down and cut off your head. Today I will give the carcasses of the Philistine army to the birds of the air and the beasts of the earth, **and the whole world will know that there is a God in Israel.** All those gathered here will know that it is not by sword or spear that the LORD saves; for the battle is the LORD's, and he will give all of you into our hands"* (1 Samuel 17:45-47, emphasis mine).

Although David faced a natural foe, he understood that the power to defeat his foe rested in the spirit realm. He knew that the Lord doesn't rescue by the sword or the spear. The Lord said: *"Not by might nor by power, but by my Spirit"* (Zechariah 4:6). So David invoked the name of the Lord for power. He also understood that the purpose of his victory was for the glory of the Lord, not his own. Victory would mean that the whole world would know that there was a God in Israel.

By this same guarantee of victory, you'll subdue and rule over the very things that attempt to establish dominion over you. Those who try to oppress you will have to restore all that they steal from you. Then you will take your would-be oppressors captive and rule over them. God will give you wisdom to overcome the enemy's devices and take him captive!

Nations will take them and bring them to their own place. And the house of Israel will possess the nations as menservants and maidservants in the LORD's land. They will make captives of their captors and rule over their oppressors (Isaiah 14:2).

For I will give you words and wisdom that none of your adversaries will be able to resist or contradict (Luke 21:15).

When you're fully committed to the Lord, problems certainly will come up, but you will have the ability to rule over them. You have the power and authority to rule over all of the earth. If you're not ruling over your circumstances, they're ruling over you. Moreover, if that happens, then you aren't operating with God's divine potential that is within you.

Choose this day to rise up to the level God created for you!

DIVINE POTENTIAL POWER POINTS

Now reviewing what you have learned from the Word of Almighty God, the Creator of the universe:

You have endless empowerment because:

- You were created in His image and likeness; you have the capacity for God to dwell in you.
- God gave you His Word of blessings; you are continually being blessed.

You have been given five divine directives:

- **Be Fruitful**—You will bear fruit and be productive in all that you do.

- **Multiply**—Multiplication, not simply addition, will occur in your life.
- **Replenish**—You can improve anything.
- **Subdue**—You will resist every attack against you.
- **Take Dominion**—You have the authority from God.

Now know that your victory is assured because God is with you to bring it to pass!

A Divine Potential Prayer for You!

Lord, help me begin to walk in the authority You have given me to be fruitful, multiply, replenish, subdue and have dominion over the earth. You have created me in Your image and likeness; therefore, I shall live a victorious life. I ask that my life will be so filled with your presence that others will see You in me as I advance towards my divine potential. Then, as they inquire of me regarding my victory, I may give You all the glory. In Jesus' name I pray. Amen.

CHAPTER 4

Transformation Exercises

The Double V and the MAP!

Now as we prepare to go forward, we must learn to develop some disciplines so that we may achieve our full divine potential. Exercises in the spirit, just like exercises in the natural, require effort. It is understandable that whenever you undertake the effort to do something that is going to give you the ability to defeat satan and his demons, he is going to challenge you. He will not sit idly by and allow you to grow strong in the Word of God and seize your divine potential without trying to stop you. He knows it is easier to stop a seed from growing than it is to push over a tree. Because he will resist you, recognize it will require some work and effort on your part, but don't be discouraged. Your labor will not be in vain.

We are all willing to work (well, *most* of us are) in order to make a living. Most people work approximately forty hours a week. They work for a human employer in exchange for wages. These wages are limited with regard to the returns they provide. For instance, the dollars you earn cannot be eaten, or heal your body, or give you peace. Of course, you might say that money will go a long way toward accomplishing some of these things. However, the truth of the matter is that wages are temporal. Many people do not even make enough money to find any happiness, joy, or peace, yet they still work for such insufficiency.

God says:

> *Come, all you who are thirsty, come to the waters; and you who have no money, come, buy and eat! Come, buy wine and milk without money and without cost. Why spend money on what is not bread, and your labor on what does not satisfy? Listen, listen to me, and eat what is good, and your soul will delight in the richest of fare. Give ear and come to me; hear me, that your soul may live. I will make an everlasting covenant with you, my faithful love promised to David* (Isaiah 55:1-3).

God is encouraging us not to just spend our time trying to make a living by working for money, but to come to Him and spend our time learning of Him. Then we can experience true life and living. He says we should use our labor to buy from Him and then we will eat what is good. Our souls—our joy and peace and happiness—will be rich. If we will labor for that which does not satisfy under earthly employers, how much more should we labor for that which is complete under our heavenly Father? Only God can fulfill our greatest needs and desires.

How do you illustrate to God that you are willing to serve Him? You do so in the same way you prove to an earthly employer that you desire to work for him or her: you develop the skills and resources that will benefit the profitability of his or her company. Likewise, you must develop the skills and resources that will illustrate to God your commitment to serving Him. This chapter will help you do that.

Proving Your Will

Adam, with his freedom to choose, denied God's right to set his boundaries and crossed over into areas that were forbidden by God. His rebellion against God meant that he would not have Him as Lord over his life. Consequently, he would no longer have God's protection from a substandard way of living nor would he have the certainty of a superior life-style that had been guaranteed by God.

Now it's your turn to exert your free will and choose. You can accept God's boundaries for your life through Jesus Christ or you can live life your own way. If you agree to submit to God's Lordship over your life, you have His power available to you within the parameters He has set for you.

In order to assist you in achieving your divine potential, God has given me two exercises to help propel you forward. If you'll put these simple exercises to daily use, you'll find yourself being transformed day by day. The purpose of these exercises is to help focus your mind on submitting to the will of God and presenting your body to Him as a living sacrifice. (See Romans 12:1-2.)

God is your Creator, and He is all-powerful. However, He still desires for you to willingly submit to Him. I cannot repeat this often enough: God will not override your free will. He will submit to your will just as He desires for you to submit to His. Therefore, you must be careful not to negate the will of God for your life by exercising your own will. It is important that you submit to His will daily, thereby proclaiming Him as Lord over your life.

These two exercises will help you come into agreement with God's will for your life. They'll enable you to manifest God's purpose in natural reality. As you begin to activate these principles in your life, they'll keep you on the right path and enable you to prove God's perfect will.

I call these two exercises **"the Double V"** and **"the MAP"**! They are Transformation Exercises. As you practice them, your focus will be on God's Word, and this will automatically transform your life.

These are simple exercises, but if they are practiced consistently, the results will be truly astounding, even if they are subtle at first. You will be planting the seed of the Word of God in your heart, and as His Word is continuously nursed by your consistency and faithfulness, it will produce a crop that will bring glory to God.

Exercise #1—The Double V

This exercise consists of two words that begin with the letter "V." The words are self-explanatory. You are to use these words to do exactly what they say in regard to the Word of God that you are studying. As you do this, the Holy Spirit, our Partner, will reveal other thoughts and ideas for you to research in God's Word.

The first **"V"** stands for **Visualize.** As you study the Word of God and find the scripture that is dear to your heart, see yourself in that scripture and visualize the situation or circumstance that God will bring to pass in your life. If the scripture says that God will comfort you, visualize yourself being comforted in the arms of God. If the scripture says that He will protect you, see yourself being protected. If the scripture says that you will be triumphant, see yourself in the role of a conqueror. If it says that you are healed, then see yourself as being healed. See yourself doing that which you have been told you cannot do. This exercise may require some creativity on your part, but it doesn't have to be perfect. The important thing is to visualize what God says that He will do for you.

Consider other examples as follows:

- Visualize yourself being created in God's image in as many ways as you can.
- Visualize obeying the Word of God (studying the Bible, praying, loving others, etc.)
- Visualize being honest and dealing with people justly. Imagine others' response to your honesty. Picture God being pleased with you.
- Visualize being part of the Body of Christ, working together with other believers for God's glory.
- Visualize yourself as a child of God, coming to Him for advice, love, and communication.
- Visualize God responding to you and providing solutions to your problems.
- Visualize yourself as a caterpillar that is being transformed into a butterfly. See the Word of God working within you right now, changing you, and teaching you how to soar above the earth's boundaries.
- Visualize being blessed and having the power to bless others.
- Visualize being fruitful and realize that whatever you do (ministry, work, relationships, hobbies, etc.), you add value to it.
- Visualize multiplying, teaching, and leading others (family, friends, and strangers) to Christ, reproducing God's image.

- Visualize subduing and taking dominion, facing your troubles and taking authority over them. Picture them as being under your feet! (See 1 Corinthians 15:27-28.)
- Visualize achieving your divine potential and achieving the goals and heights in life that God has set before you. Visualize yourself becoming the person God says you are.
- Visualize God's power being made available to you when you need it.

Visualize yourself in the way God sees you. When God wanted Abraham to realize how much land He was going to give him, He gave him something to visualize. See how God inspired Abraham:

> *Lift up your eyes from where you are and look north and south, east and west. All the land that you see I will give to you and your offspring forever* (Genesis 13:14-15).

When God wanted to give Abraham a vision of the nation he was to become,

> *He took him outside and said, "Look up at the heavens and count the stars—if indeed you can count them." Then he said to him, "So shall your offspring be"* (Genesis 15:5).

Time and time again, God gave Abraham something to help him visualize what his future would be. Here's another case in point:

> *I will surely bless you and make your descendants as numerous as the stars in the sky and as the sand on the seashore. Your descendants will take possession of the cities of their enemies* (Genesis 22:17).

What has God been showing you? Visualize that image over and over in your mind. Remember, without a vision, the people perish.

> *Where there is no vision, the people perish* (Proverbs 29:18, KJV).

Therefore, if you can have a visualization (a revelation) of a thing, you can acquire what it shows you and flourish!

As you work out this first "V" in your own life, know and believe in your heart all that God's Word says about you. In this way you will see yourself accomplishing things about which others cannot even dream.

The second 'V" stands for **Verbalize.** After all, God said, "*Out of the abundance of the heart the mouth speaketh*" (Matthew 12:34, KJV). Now you are to speak what you have read from the Word of God. You are to do this over and over again. Find the scripture that gives you the authority over any obstacle in your path and say it out loud again and again and again. You are created in the image and likeness of God. Imitate your Father. Remember, God's words created the universe. All things in existence are obedient to the spoken Word of God. As you speak scripture, the words impact the atmosphere. That impact alters your environment.

Being in the image of your Father, you too can call ". . . *things that are not as though they were*" (Romans 4:17). Your spoken words cause the air around you to vibrate, and they generate a force that can be scientifically recorded and documented. You have felt the force of sound waves in many different ways. There are sound waves generated in music that are pleasing, stimulating, exciting, peaceful, or invigorating. Sound waves can also be distracting, annoying, dissonant, and destructive. At high frequency, sound can even shatter glass. At low frequency, such as the vibration created by a deep sub woofer, a rumble that is so powerful that it can crack walls and destroy hearing takes place. In fact, such sounds are used as weapons and devices of torture.

Always remember that your ". . . *tongue has the power of life and death*" (Proverbs 18:21). Therefore, at all times be sure to speak life, not death.

Mark 11:22-23 explains that when you have faith in God, you can tell a mountain (a particular trouble or difficulty) to throw itself into the sea (be removed from your presence) and it will be done:

> *"Have faith in God," Jesus answered. "I tell you the truth, if anyone says to this mountain, 'Go, throw yourself*

into the sea,' and does not doubt in his heart but believes that what he says will happen, it will be done for him."

Another interesting encounter we find in scripture involves Ezekiel. God tells the prophet to actually speak to some dry bones. Here we can examine what spoken words can do:

The hand of the Lord was upon me, and he brought me out by the Spirit of the Lord and set me in the middle of a valley; it was full of bones. He led me back and forth among them, and I saw a great many bones on the floor of the valley, bones that were very dry. He asked me, "Son of man, can these bones live?" I said, "O Sovereign Lord, you alone know"

Then he said to me, "Prophesy to these bones and say to them, 'Dry bones, hear the word of the Lord! This is what the Sovereign Lord says to these bones: I will make breath enter you, and you will come to life. I will attach tendons to you and make flesh come upon you and cover you with skin; I will put breath in you, and you will come to life. Then you will know that I am the Lord.'"

So I prophesied as I was commanded. And as I was prophesying, there was a noise, a rattling sound, and the bones came together, bone to bone. I looked, and tendons and flesh appeared on them and skin covered them, but there was no breath in them.

Then he said to me, "Prophesy to the breath; prophesy, son of man, and say to it, 'This is what the Sovereign Lord says: Come from the four winds, O breath, and breathe into these slain, that they may live.'" So I prophesied as he commanded me, and breath entered them; they came to life and stood up on their feet—a vast army (Ezekiel 37:1-10).

Remember, God called the unseen into existence by His spoken Word. You can alter your physical world with vibrations from sound that are in line with the will and Word of God. Your world awaits your verbal agreement with the Word of God to bring His will to pass in your life.

The more you speak, the clearer you envision yourself as God says you are. The more you picture it, the more you'll say it! The world and circumstances will never be able to move you off course.

Exercise #2—MAP!

This exercise is another life-transforming discipline. *MAP!* is an acronym for these words: **Meditate, Apply** and **Perform.** It is a road map for your life.

1) **Meditate** upon God's Word in order to be able to know His voice.

2) **Apply** God's Word to your life.

3) **Perform** what you have learned from His Word

MEDITATE

Meditation is an almost-forgotten discipline in the Christian Church, but it is a practice that draws us closer to the Lord. When we meditate upon His Word, it transforms our lives so that we are more like Him.

What does "meditation" actually mean? It means: "to murmur, speak, moan, mutter, babble, talk, sing, discuss, or ponder verbally." God told Joshua to meditate on His Word both day and night. God said that his way would be prosperous and successful if he did so. (See Joshua 1:8.) So shall it be for you. Meditation places the Word of God in your heart. It is a deliberate process of communing with God by quietly studying, singing, and reflecting on His Word again and again—over and over, and over again—and over again. In this way you are strengthening the Word of God in your heart, mind and soul.

The process of meditation is like a sheep's digestion process. When a sheep first swallows, the food passes to the first of its four stomachs. Later, the sheep brings up the digesting food as "cud" and chews it again. Again the sheep swallows, passing the cud to the second stomach. The sheep brings it back up a third time, chews it, and swallows it again. Eventually the cud will go through all four of its stomachs.

In the same way that the sheep is nourished by food, you receive sustenance from the Word of God. Jesus explained, *"Man does not live on bread alone, but on every word that comes from the mouth of God"* (Matthew 4:4). As the sheep chews its cud, you, too, chew on God's Word. Meditating on His Word maintains your spiritual health and elevates you to receive revelation from Him.

God's Purpose for Meditating on His Word

Meditation helps you have the mind of God. It disciplines your thinking so that you may know God better. God said:

> *"For my thoughts are not your thoughts, neither are your ways my ways," declares the LORD. "As the heavens are higher than the earth, so are my ways higher than your ways and my thoughts than your thoughts"* (Isaiah 55:8-9).

Meditating on God's Word renews your mind and transforms your life. It allows you to replicate the mind of Christ within you. (See Romans 12:2 and 1 Corinthians 2:16.) Likewise, it enables you to bring every thought under obedience to His Word repeatedly until you automatically think, say, and do it. It is then that you experience Kingdom living and enter a heavenly realm of blessings in the here and now!

Satan knows the power that comes from meditation on God's Word. He also knows that when you grow in the knowledge of God's Word and faith, you are able to subdue and take dominion over him. His greatest fear is that this will happen and you will multiply your knowledge and faith to other men and women, inflicting severe and heavy casualties upon his kingdom and his activities. His purpose, therefore, is to thwart you from obtaining your divine potential. He will do all he can to prevent the Word of God from richly dwelling in you. Resist him by submitting to God's revelation of His Word in your life. Then declare God's Word over satan's lies, which are *always* contrary to the truth.

Be very careful about how you think. If you allow it, your thoughts can cause you to separate yourself from God and negate the force of His power being manifested in your life. Your thoughts can also cause you to turn your focus away from God and toward a worldly mentality. This is why we're told to take captive every thought that is contrary to the Word of God. (See 2 Corinthians 10:5.)

The world's system and its way of life continually bombard you with information that is contrary to the Word of God in order to get you to succumb to its temptation. This happens everywhere, and it is all around you. Think about how the radio, television, billboards, and newspapers continually repeat information. Marketers and salespeople know that if they can affect your thinking, they can affect how you spend your money. With repetition, they are able to convince you that you *need* things that you don't need at all. Worse still, they distract you from focusing on the things you really should be focusing on.

On the other hand, repetition can work to your advantage when it's applied to meditating on God's Word. This same process can alter your actions internally and externally to focus on things that will enhance your life for the glory of God. God's Word is a spiritual force. Stop now and think: it was Him speaking His Word that created the universe and all that's in it. It was by the force of His Spirit that man became a living being. Thus, by meditating and speaking His Word, you have the power to alter your universe and, by the force of His Spirit, He will give renewed life to your mortal body!

When your thoughts are focused on God's Word, He's obligated to direct your path into the way of knowledge that is necessary to accomplish His will in your life. The amount of time you give to meditating on God's Word is in direct proportion to the increase you receive, multiplied back to you.

Your Transformation

In the Book of John we read:

> *"In the beginning was the Word, and the Word was with God, and the Word was God"* (John 1:1). In a later passage

we read, *"The Word became flesh and made his dwelling among us. We have seen his glory, the glory of the One and Only, who came from the Father, full of grace and truth"* (John 1:14).

From these verses we know that in the very beginning, there was God, and we learn that God and His Word are the same. We know also that God/the Word put on the form of a man and was born into the world. In other words, God/the Word put on a clay body. This form or clay body was Jesus. As you and I put on clothes, we realize that the life is not in the clothes, but the clothes envelop our lives (the life). The frame or form has no worth. That which is on the inside is all that has value.

Therefore, it was the Word in Jesus that was the power of God to do works on the earth. This power was not found in the Man. The Man died, but the Word inside resurrected the Man to life again. Such is also the case with you. Do not allow your thoughts regarding your physical form to hinder the work of the power of the Word inside of you. The same power that was in Christ Jesus is also at work in you. *"And we also thank God continually because, when you received the Word of God, which you heard from us, you accepted it not as the word of men, but as it actually is, the Word of God, which is at work in you who believe"* (1 Thessalonians 2:13).

> *And we, who with unveiled faces all reflect the Lord's glory, are being transformed into his likeness with ever-increasing glory, which comes from the Lord, who is the Spirit* (2 Corinthians 3:18).

Take note, as you meditate on God's Word, you will be transformed into His likeness. The ever-increasing glory is the ever-increasing power of God that you reflect as a result of His work in you. The end result is the fullness of your divine potential.

> *"Consider carefully what you hear,"* he continued. *"With the measure you use, it will be measured to you—and even more"* (Mark 4:24).

Another reason for meditation is so that you may know the voice of the Lord when He speaks to you throughout each day. There are many spirits and many voices that constantly call to you and talk to you, pretending to be the voice of the Lord, to lead you astray. Sorting out the authentic voice of God is a matter of practice. Meditating on His Word helps you to know and recognize His voice.

Let's look at what He told Joshua when it was time for him to lead the Israelites into the Promised Land after he took over the leadership of the people upon the death of Moses. God gives him encouraging words to help him accomplish the awesome work that was before him. He repeatedly tells him to be strong and courageous. (This is the very same encouragement you need today in order to accomplish the impossible in your life.) He tells Joshua the importance of meditating upon His Word and the results of doing so.

> *Be strong and courageous, because you will lead these people to inherit the land I swore to their forefathers to give them. Be strong and very courageous. Be careful to obey all the law my servant Moses gave you; do not turn from it to the right or to the left, that you may be successful wherever you go. Do not let this Book of the Law depart from your mouth; meditate on it day and night, so that you may be careful to do everything written in it. Then you will be prosperous and successful. Have I not commanded you? Be strong and courageous. Do not be terrified; do not be discouraged, for the Lord your God will be with you wherever you go* (Joshua 1:6-9).

God made it clear that meditating on His Word would bring Joshua success in all that he did. Therefore, God encouraged him to make Bible meditation a daily part of his life.

Have you ever noticed that God never condemns anyone for thinking about or focusing on Him too much? In fact, He encourages us to think on Him and what He has to say. The more you think about it, the more it gets into your heart. Then, as Jesus told us, out of the overflow of the heart, the mouth speaks. (See Matthew 12:34.) Once again, this prepares you for your verbalization to have an impact on your environment. Jesus also says, *"By your words you will be acquitted, and by your words you will be condemned"* (Matthew 12:37). Your words are tremendously effective. Paul puts it this way:

> *For it is with your heart that you believe and are justified, and it is with your mouth that you confess and are saved* (Romans 10:10).

In other words, you will speak what is in your heart. Your meditation gets into your heart and you speak it. Because the Word of God is life, you speak life into your life. Life upon life is abundant life.

David tells us in Psalm 1 that if we meditate on God's Word, whatever we do will prosper. He also says, *"Your commands make me wiser than my enemies, for they are ever with me. I have more insight than all my teachers, <u>for I meditate</u> on your statutes. I have more understanding than the elders, for I obey your precepts"* (Psalm 119:98-100, emphasis mine).

What tremendous gain is given by us simply meditating upon what God has said. Here is what the wisest man who ever lived said regarding the Word of God:

> *My son, do not forget my teaching, but keep my commands in your heart, for they will prolong your life many years and bring you prosperity* (Proverbs 3:1-2).

> *My son, pay attention to what I say; listen closely to my words. Do not let them out of your sight, keep them within your heart; for they are life to those who find them and health to a man's whole body* (Proverbs 4:20-22).

Find It and Live

Now, open your Bible and find scriptures that reveal what you need most. Remember, all scripture is God-breathed. All scripture is life to you for both health and prosperity. All of this is given to you for the glory of God so that you may obtain your divine potential and serve Him in the earth.

Next, memorize it so that you know it well. Don't be afraid to learn long passages. Even though memorizing might seem difficult at first, you will find that it gets easier. The more you practice, the more you will be able to memorize. Remember that God's Word is life. It will not return to Him void. Therefore, memorizing the Word is well worth the effort.

Write out the scripture you're focusing on and mark the key words. Break it into sections to help you see it more clearly. Then speak it over and over again, thinking about each concept it presents. Because man does not live by bread alone, but by every word that proceeds out of the mouth of God, think and meditate on each word. Make it personal. See a picture of it in your mind and see it happening for you in your life. Remember this: no matter how much you meditate on a passage, you will never get to the bottom, to the top, or to the end of all that God can reveal to you about it.

One of the most marvelous things about meditating on God's Word is that the Holy Spirit will be your Teacher, and He will reveal things to you—things you never knew before. *"Oh, the depth of the riches of the wisdom and knowledge of God! How unsearchable his judgments, and his paths beyond tracing out!"* (Romans 11:33).

How wonderful this is! If there is something you want in life and it seems difficult to attain, you don't even have to think long or worry about how you're going to get it. Simply find the promise in the Word of God and let God's Word show you the way. Find it and meditate on it. As you meditate, you are hiding God's Word in your heart. It is from your heart that the issues in your life will flow—and you will prosper.

The Process of Meditation on God's Word—Ten Steps

1. Set aside a quiet time to be alone with God.
- Plan for mornings or evenings, whichever works best for you.
- Always keep your appointed time.
- Daniel met with the Lord three times a day.
- Jesus often sought a quiet place to be alone with God.

2. Ask for the Holy Spirit's help.

- He will reveal the mind of God to you. (See 1 Corinthians 2:9-12.)
- He will help you in your weaknesses. (See Romans 8:26-27.)
- He will teach you spiritual things. (See 1 Corinthians 2:13.)

3. Search the Word of God.

- The Word will help you overcome circumstances.
- Use various versions of the Bible, books, tapes, and aids to understand Scripture.
- Search the Word for promises, especially those dealing with things close to your heart.
- *"All Scripture is God-breathed"* (2 Timothy 3:16-17); thus the Bible is life to you.

4. Review the passage over again and over again.

- Read Scriptures, subjects, and stories in the Bible that are of interest to you.
- Study for related topics in the Bible—cross reference them.
- Look for meanings in the original texts (Hebrew for the Old Testament and Greek for the New Testament).
- Study maps or draw out visuals to clarify your understanding.
- Analyze, ponder, and think about it. Studying God's Word is the highest form of worship.

5. Destroy any thought(s) that are contrary to the Word.

- Any reasoning or arguments.
- Any pride or arrogance.
- Any self-pity or guilt.
- Anything " ... *that sets itself up against the knowledge of God"* (2 Corinthians 10:4-5).

6. Write it out and memorize it. (Read Deuteronomy 6:6-9.)

- Keep the Word in you; lock it in your mind.
- Underline key words on which you will meditate further.

- Memorize it well, even long passages.
- Sing it, put it into a melody.
- Include family and friends, and others.
- Teach them.
- Talk about it to them.
- Study with them.
- Play memory games.
- Sing songs.

7. Verbalize it.

- Do word studies—speak them aloud repeatedly.
- Emphasize a different word each time you review, and meditate on it in the context of scripture. Look at Psalm 1:3. Here is an example:
- **He**
- He **is**
- He is **like**
- He is like **a tree**
- He is like a tree **planted**

(Notice a person does not plant himself. He *is* planted. The verb **planted** (Hebrew: *shatal*) indicates that the godly person doesn't take root haphazardly or under his own initiative. He is planted by God in order that he may bring **forth fruit.** The purpose of God's planting a person in the fertile soil is always the production of fruit. (cf. Ephesians 2:8b-10; Colossians 1:9b-10). This speaks to where you are in life.

- He is like a tree planted by **streams**

(This is a plural word that means "more than one." It refers to fellowshipping with others in a church that teaches the Word. It is not good for you to be alone. God desires for you to fellowship with other believers.)

- He is like a tree planted by streams **of water**. (Water refers to the Word constantly flowing and flourishing in our lives.)

- He is like a tree planted by streams of water, which **yields/ produces its fruit.** (Being fruitful and multiplying are certain.)
- He is like a tree planted by streams of water, which yields its fruit **in season.** (There's a time when it'll manifest. Therefore, do not become weary in well doing)
- He is like a tree planted by streams of water, which yields its fruit in season and whose **leaf does not wither.** (It's replenished.)
- He is like a tree planted by streams of water, which yields its fruit in season and whose leaf does not wither. **Whatever he does prospers.** (He subdues and has dominion.)

8. Visualize it.
- See a picture of the passage in your mind.
- See yourself meditating on the Word day and night. Then you become like a tree planted by the streams. Visualize yourself planted in a good church. You are fellowshipping with other children of God. God blesses you with wise counsel and friends. See fruit in areas of your life that are lacking. The *rhema* Word of God continues to flow in your life daily. Visualize everything you touch, do, or speak improving. Whatever you do prospers.
- Visualize whatever God speaks to you.
- Visualize praying with God, and visualize all hindering obstacles and mountains moving out of your way.
- Remember what God said to Abraham regarding the stars and sand, how numerous his offspring would be.

9. Make it personal.
Apply the Word to you personally. Begin to declare the Word, not your situation.
- Know that God speaks personally to His people.
- "He who belongs to God hears what God says" (John 8:47).
- This means that God is saying something to His people. There's life when God speaks to you! If God were to stop speaking, the universe would cease to exist.

- Think of the power in God's Word.
- The Word will accomplish what God desires for it to accomplish. (See Isaiah 55:11.)
- God's angels do His commandments and carry out His spoken Word. (See Psalm 103:20.) They'll carry it out for you if you speak it.

10. Stay on course.
- Never grow tired of speaking God's Word over and over again.
- God is eternal, and His Word is eternal. You'll never come to a place where you know all the scriptures. There's perpetual meaning in each verse. (See Romans 11:33.)
- All day, morning, and night meditate on God's Word. Work on scripture in the shower, at lunch, before you go to bed. Put it on your refrigerator, on the mirror, even as your screen-saver.
- Don't worry about any problems you have; find their solutions in the Word and meditate on it!
- Continue to follow the **Ten Steps on Meditation**.

APPLY

The next word in "the MAP! Exercise" speaks to learning to apply God's Word to your life. One of the major problems in the Christian Church is that we have a great deal of knowledge in the form of godliness, but we deny its power. We conveniently pick and choose what part of God's Word we're going to believe. But God's Word is not just for one generation or for one culture. God's Word is eternal and universal. There is nothing new under the sun. What has been will be again, what has been done will be done again. (See Ecclesiastes 1:9.) Whatever you encounter in life, God has already given you a solution for it.

Find It! God has an answer for every situation you encounter. He says in Psalm 119:105, *"Your word is a lamp to my feet and a light for my path."* His Word is a guide for your life that will lead you in all your endeavors. All things change, but God's Word never changes. There is only one interpretation, but there are many applications.

There is danger in misapplying God's Word. Therefore, you must study to show yourself approved unto God and rightly divide the Word of truth. (See 2 Timothy 2:15.) Seek out the whole counsel of the Lord and then apply that Word to your life. It doesn't matter what you see; all that matters is what God says.

As you apply God's Word to your life, humble yourself. His Word is not for those who think themselves to be wise. God will use things that you think are foolish in order to accomplish His purpose. There is no power in your humanity. There is no real wisdom in you. Therefore, commit to know nothing except what God says. When you think you have a conclusion to a matter, test that conclusion by what His Word says. Don't let your past teaching or your thoughts get in the way. satan has manipulated this world's system to keep you ignorant of your divine potential. Conform to God's Word alone.

There are those who will fail in life because they are too proud to change according to the Word and allow it to have root in their lives. They thrive on what they think God has told them by special revelation. They speak what they say the Spirit has told them. They speak about the dreams. But none of what they say can be found in the Bible. They will contradict what God has said in His written Word by saying what they believe. Keep away from these people, no matter how well-intentioned they are. If what they say isn't confirmed in the Bible, then it is false.

If God says a thing about a subject, He will say it in many places so there is no room for doubt. He tells us that it's on the testimony of two or three witnesses that the truth will be known. Therefore, research all God has to say about a subject in His written Word, and then you will not have to interpret it. Learn to compare scripture with scripture. Don't decide what to do by just reading a single scripture; back it up with others. Something that is not clear in one place may be clear elsewhere.

When I was young, I believed that it was acceptable for a man to have more than one wife. After all, in the Bible it reveals that many men had more than one wife and this, I thought, justified polygamy. However, by rightly dividing the Word, I realized that this was not God's plan. This was an action that was taken by man. I noticed that Adam only had one wife. God did not find it necessary to give him Eve, Diane, Susan, Janie, and Mary Sue. Further, I realized that Noah had only one wife, and he was a righteous man. Job only had one, and he was righteous. Abraham messed all of us up by taking Hagar. David started running into trouble by having more than one. Without doubt, God was making it clear that it was not His will for a man to have more than one wife.

If God's Word is clear, don't use your brain, because it's incapable of understanding much about God's ways. He doesn't think as we do. It doesn't matter what you see, hear, or feel. All that matters is what God says. When you trust Him, He guides and corrects you. Meditate on the Word of God and then apply the Word you have studied to your life.

PERFORM

The next part of "the MAP! Exercise" is performing God's Word. The power of God grows in people who are bold enough to perform it. The more you are faithful with the Word you know, the more God will give you and the more you will grow. The more you grow, the more you will know. The more you know, the more you will be shown the power and grace of God.

Remember what God said to Joshua, " ... *that you may be careful to do everything written in it. Then you will be prosperous and successful*" (Joshua 1:8b). What's the simple interpretation? Perform God's Word and you will be successful! Not only will you be successful, but God says you will be prosperous, as well. This is His promise to you. You must do more than meditate and be able to relate His Word to your life. You must do what it says. The power of God to achieve your divine potential only manifests itself when you do what God says to do. And you will!

God says that if you are willing and obedient, you will eat the best from the land. (See Isaiah 1:19.) It takes courage to be obedient, but when you are obedient, you reap great returns. The world will make this difficult for you. People might say that you're stuck up, behind the times, in another world, out of step, or politically incorrect. Honestly, it might seem easier just to become a follower than to go against family and friends and risk criticism and scorn. Producing fruit for the Kingdom is a difficult thing, but you have clear instructions and plenty of support. Jesus says you must deny yourself and take up your cross and follow Him. (See Matthew 16:24.)

Joshua needed strength and encouragement not because he would be fighting an enemy in the world, but because it was so difficult to obey God when the world was rebelling against Him.

This difficulty in obedience is warfare in your head, and satan will yield no ground easily to you. When you have achieved one victory, there will be another battle. But let these words comfort you as you seek to perform what God would have you to do.

> *A righteous man may have many troubles, but the Lord delivers him from them all* (Psalm 34:19).

Again, we see God's willingness to assist you when you stand on His Word and apply it properly.

Performing God's Word means doing ALL, not part of it. He tells Joshua, *"...do not turn from it to the right or to the left"* (Joshua 1:7). This means strict adherence to the Word of God. Success comes from doing God's Word. God is looking for people who are fully committed to Him and seek to do His will so that He might show himself strong for them. He is looking for *you*. God is eager to bless you. He wants to help you achieve your divine potential. You prove yourself qualified for it as you continuously perform His Word.

Why does God have you meditate upon His Word and command you to be careful to apply it? So that you may be prosperous and successful in everything you do. It is all about doing, doing, doing—not just talking, talking, talking. That is why Jesus speaks so often about fruit-bearing. Remember, you have a divine directive to be fruitful. That means you are to produce and perform.

Solomon was considered the wisest man who ever lived. Look at one of the reasons for his wisdom:

> *When the time drew near for David to die, he gave a charge to Solomon his son. "I am about to go the way of all the earth," he said. "So be strong, show yourself a man, and observe what the Lord your God requires: Walk in his ways, and keep his decrees and commands, his laws and*

requirements, as written in the Law of Moses, so that you may prosper in all you do and wherever you go" (1 Kings 2:1-3).

Solomon was encouraged to perform the Word of God. Obedience always means increase in your life. To be successful, you must perform God's Word.

Some people think that going to church will save them. They are mistaken. It's not enough. A lot of church members go through hell in life and then experience it in the afterlife, as well. Jesus said that many will call him Lord, but only those who perform His Word are truly His servants. It doesn't matter how many scriptures churchgoers can quote, how loudly they sing, how well they pray, or how much they speak in tongues. If they don't live the life, or perform what God says to do, they will miss out on the blessings of God.

> *Do not merely listen to the word, and so deceive yourselves. Do what it says* (James 1:22).

If all you do is *listen* to the Word, you deceive yourself. To *hear* the Word means both to *listen* and *obey*. These are important distinctions that bear repeating: to *hear* means to *listen* and *obey*. When God reveals something to you, act as though it's reality, even if it's not (at the moment). In other words, show your faith by what you do.

The true measure of success is directly proportional to the diligence you apply to obeying the Word of God!

When you believe that the Word of God is true, you act upon it. But if you're not acting upon it, you need to ask yourself some questions:

1. Why don't I believe God's Word?

2. What's hindering me? (Is it a lack of the Word of God, or is it thoughts, people, the past, or circumstances?)

3. In what areas am I being deceived?

4. How can I start being who I really am—in words, actions, thoughts, and deeds?

Now speak, memorize, and meditate on these scriptures until the Word in them becomes the Word in you:

> *Do not merely listen to the word, and so deceive yourselves. Do what it says. Anyone who listens to the word but does not do what it says is like a man who looks at his face in a mirror and, after looking at himself, goes away and immediately forgets what he looks like"* (James 1:22-24).

INSTEAD, BE THE PERSON WHO . . .

> *... looks intently into the perfect law that gives freedom, and continues to do this, not forgetting what he has heard, but doing it—he will be blessed in what he does. If anyone considers himself religious and yet does not keep a tight rein on his tongue, he deceives himself and his religion is worthless* (James 1:25-26).

Summary

Use these exercises to strengthen your knowledge of God's Word. His Word will transform your life so that you are equipped to contain the fullness of His power. Remember, He created you in His image and likeness so that He might live inside you.

These exercises prepare you to receive the Master of the universe, Almighty God.

YOUR DIVINE POTENTIAL POWER POINTS

Continue Your Two Exercises:
    Exercise #1—VISUALIZE and VERBALIZE
    Exercise #2—MAP!
- Meditate
- Apply
- Perform

Make the decision to know who you really are and commit yourself to it! Don't forget what you've read and received about who you are. Turn and face God. Look intently at the Word to **realize** who He says you are, then **VISUALIZE, VERBALIZE,** and **MAP!** (Meditate on it, Apply it, Perform it). Through these means you are getting closer to seizing your divine potential.

Now, Visualize!
Now, Verbalize!
Now, Meditate!
Now, Apply!
Now, Perform!

〰〰〰〰

A Divine Potential Prayer for You!

Lord, help me to see myself through Your eyes so that I may speak Your words over my life. I will meditate on Your Word, fix my eyes on Your ways and obey Your commands continually, forever and ever. Thank you for allowing your Word to be a lamp unto my feet and a light unto my path. Though I may stumble or even fall, I know You will lift me up and lead me to my full divine potential. For this confidence I thank you. In Jesus' name I pray. Amen.

SECTION TWO

INTRODUCTION

Five Performance Principles
for Seizing Your Divine Potential

My people are destroyed from lack of knowledge
(Hosea 4:6).

As Hosea says, lack of knowledge destroys us. Indeed, ignorance
of the magnificent mandate God gave us—divine potential—has
prevented many of us from living up to the standards He designed for
us. In Section One, we revealed our source of endless empowerment
and the divine directives that God gave to us in the very beginning.
We came to understand that all God established in the beginning for
all creation remains until today. The things that He commanded for
the universe in the beginning are final. His Word does not change.
Therefore, the divine potential that God gave to Adam is still
available to us today. In fact, the potential is even greater because
Christ is now with the Father. Jesus has said that we will even do
greater things than He did. (See John 14:12.) And let us remember
also that the great works of the first covenant were merely a shadow
of the reality of the works we should do under the New Covenant. It
is still God's will for men and women to fulfill their divine potential,
and He will work with anyone who desires to achieve it.

Although it is God's will for you to fulfill your divine potential,
you must be in agreement with God. You exhibit that will by
developing your faith. Faith pleases God and causes Him to reward
you with an ever-increasing measure of His power to do His will.

We have learned that by lack of faith, it's possible to negate His will for someone's life. We must do battle with thoughts that limit our faith and hinder the force of His will from being active in our lives. We align ourselves with the will of God so that His power will work through us to fulfill His purposes.

Armed with the knowledge you now have, you can activate the power God has given you to seize your divine potential through disciplines and routines called "Performance Principles." All you have to do is to follow His instructions, which are made clear in the Word of God.

Now I will walk you through the **Five Performance Principles to Seize Your Divine Potential.**

Performance Principle #1: **Find Out Who You Really Are.** Learn who you really are, not the person you and others think or believe you are. We will remove the mask you have worn for so long to reveal the *real* you, as God created you to be.

Performance Principle #2: **Align Yourself With the Word of God.** Come face-to-face with the reality of how far off course you've gone from who you really are. Properly use the tools God has given you to chart your way back on course to God's way.

Performance Principle #3: **Inquire From God What You Can Become.** Develop simple, but powerful disciplines to practice that allow you to see a unique vision of God's will for your life.

Performance Principle #4: **Take Action to Achieve Your Divine Potential.** Commit yourself to partnering with God and chart the course to your divine destiny. Fully realize the foolishness of independent thinking and the wisdom of consulting and submitting to God's authority for your life.

Performance Principle #5: **Hold Out and be Diligently Patient.** Be faithful to the end, trusting God in complete confidence to finish the work He has begun in you.

These Performance Principles have been calculated to alter your mind-set and transform you into the person God wants you to be. The end result is development of your faith. Take a look at the first letter of each Performance Principle and you will find that when you incorporate all five, you have a strong foundation in faith.

Find it—Search the scriptures to find God's Word with regard to your circumstances and to support your need. The Word is the power to overcome the adversary.

Align—Put yourself in alignment with the written Word so that you may then ask according to His Word. The important point here is to determine where you are in relation to the Word of God and then what you need to do to get in line with what God requires of you.

Inquire—Ask God what He would have you do in regards to the scripture with which you align yourself. We know "*. . . that if we ask anything according to his will, he hears us—whatever we ask— we know that we have what we asked of him*" (1 John 5:14).

Take action—Do what God has asked of you. With the confidence of the Word of God and your alignment with that Word, ask God what to do and then take action to accomplish your purpose.

Hold out—Remain persistently diligent to accomplish what God has called you to do.

This earth is not your home. You are truly a citizen of Heaven and an ambassador of the Kingdom of God. And just like any ambassador, you have diplomatic immunity from the laws of this world. Any time you experience conditions not to your liking, you have the authority to appeal to the King for His help. He stands ready to respond to your request.

Take your time and give careful thought to each principle. Each will direct you to God, who will enlighten your heart and mind with His revelation of the truth for you.

CHAPTER 5

Performance Principle Number One

Find Out Who You Really Are

Facing Spiritual Reality

Frankly, the world has lied to you all of your life about your abilities (or lack thereof!), and just like most people, you've "bought into" some or all of it. Now, it's time for truth. It's time for you to find out what God says about who you really are. His Word is truth. It is the whole truth and nothing but the truth; it is the final authority. There is nothing that could ever be more real than the Word. It is established in the heavens and cannot be changed. God has given you divine potential with tremendously awesome power. You must accept what He says about you as truth.

Correcting Your Thinking

Truth is eternal. It never changes. But our knowledge of truth is progressive. The Bible is a progressive revelation of God and the truth. As our ability to understand Him increases, so does our knowledge of Him. And, as our knowledge of God increases, so does our knowledge of the world and its challenge to the truth of the Word of God.

In order to get you to recognize and accept the truth of God, we must first purge any thinking that has been polluted by the false doctrines and teachings of the world. Use the Word of God to correct all the years of misinformation the world has fed you. His scripture says:

"For as he thinketh in his heart, so is he" (Proverbs 23:7, KJV).

This verse reveals that whatever a person thinks in his or her heart is what he or she becomes. Because of this, God instructs us, *"Keep thy heart with all diligence; for out of it are the issues of life"* (Proverbs 4:23, KJV). Meditate on this: You are created in the image of God, who created the universe from His thoughts and words. You also have the ability to create your universe and your life from your thoughts and words. This is why you are cautioned to protect your heart. For whatever is in your heart will come forth out of your mouth and affect your environment. Therefore, you must be vigilant about guarding your thoughts, because God makes it clear that what is in your heart will become reality in your life.

Jesus spoke of the importance of our thinking and how it affects our reality when He cautioned us in Matthew 5:27-28 about wrong thoughts. He said, *"You have heard that it was said, 'Do not commit adultery.' But I tell you that anyone who looks at a woman lustfully has already committed adultery with her in his heart."* James says it this way in James 1:14-15: *"Every man is tempted, when he is drawn away of his own lust, and enticed. Then when lust hath conceived, it bringeth forth sin; and sin, when it is finished, bringeth forth death"* (KJV). So, you see, if you can control your thinking, you can control your actions. And when you control your actions, you control your destiny. Develop your thinking to be in accordance with God's Word and you will advance toward your divine potential—being fruitful and productive in all your endeavors. You will triumph over adversity by His strength freely working in you.

We've already seen your potential in Genesis 1:26-28. Now, shape your thinking about yourself according to the Word of God in order to put your transformation into fulfilling the will of God into effect:

Do not conform any longer to the pattern [information] *of this world, but be transformed* [meaning transfigured, changed] *by the renewing of your mind. Then you will be able to test and approve what God's will is—His good, pleasing and perfect will* (Romans 12:2).

When your mind is renewed according to the Word of God, a transformation takes place. You are transformed progressively into the image and likeness of God, as the scripture states: " *... for as he thinks in his heart, so is he*" (Proverbs 23:7, NKJV). When your thinking is on God's Word, you are more like Him. You achieve your divine potential by qualifying yourself to contain more of the fullness of God in Christ within you.

This may seem fantastic, but it isn't any more fantastic than an ugly little caterpillar slowly crawling on a tree, eating leaves. The poor creature seems bound to a plain, unexciting life. Eventually the caterpillar forms a cocoon around itself. To the casual observer, the caterpillar is now dormant, but there's a dynamic, unseen metamorphosis going on inside the cocoon. When it opens, an entirely different creature emerges as a butterfly with wings painted in beautiful colors. Flying free, it is bound to the earth no more.

This is the way it is with you. As the Word of God is heard and placed in your heart internally, God equips you to contain the fullness of His power to be an instrument of His will on earth. All that is done on the inside is revealed on the outside. This will happen as you are faithful in the study of His Word. This process occurs progressively.

> *You were taught, with regard to your former way of life, to put off your old self, which is being corrupted by its deceitful desires; to be made new in the attitude of your minds* (Ephesians 4:22-23).

Throw off what the world has taught you. The world's corruption has kept you from achieving your divine potential. In Ephesians, this corruption is defined as "deceitful desires." Simply stated, this is thinking wrongly. All of this is seated in our minds. Again, how does the Scripture say we are to change into what God wants? We are made new in the attitude of our minds in a continual process of focusing on the Word of God.

So I tell you this, and insist on it in the Lord, that you must no longer live as the Gentiles do, in the futility of their thinking. They are darkened in their understanding and separated from the life of God because of the ignorance that is in them due to the hardening of their hearts (Ephesians 4:17-18).

We are encouraged here to stop thinking about useless things of the world—things that lead to nothing of real value. There is much knowledge in the world, but little of it is fruitful for the development of eternal gain. It is not about the things of God. Verse 18 reveals to us that even with the great knowledge of the world, many are darkened in their understanding because satan has blinded them in their hearts from knowing the real truth of the potential that is in them. They are alienated from the power of God.

Your thinking, on the other hand, must be about the right things that are revealed in the Word of God.

How you think about yourself determines how much authority and power you walk in. Consider a high-performance car with a potential speed of 200 mph. Parked, it goes nowhere. It is only when a driver mentally decides to accelerate the car to 200 mph and follows through with his decision by pushing the accelerator that the car can start to approach its potential. Likewise, the way you think will determine whether or not you will achieve your potential.

Perhaps you are not where you should be in your life right now. Perhaps you're unaware of who you are and who your Master is. Maybe you're afraid. If so, this has kept you from achieving your divine potential. You're living a life inferior to the one you were meant to have. You can't be truly happy, satisfied, and fulfilled as an eagle living the life of a chicken.

If this describes you, you are not alone. There's a severe identity crisis throughout the Body of Christ. The children of God are wrongly comparing themselves to the world and to each other. Lured by our culture and pressured by our society, a lot of people are trying to conform to what others say they should be. They are not asking the Creator what He created them to be. How foolish! They live weak, powerless, and defeated lives simply because they don't realize that they are children of God. Here is what the Apostle Peter has to say about you:

> *But you are a chosen people, a royal priesthood, a holy nation, a people belonging to God, that you may declare the praises of him who called you out of darkness into his wonderful light* (1 Peter 2:9).

satan, the Liar

Peter further cautions us in 1 Peter 5:8: "*Be self-controlled and alert. Your enemy the devil prowls around like a roaring lion looking for someone to devour.*" The Scripture says the devil prowls around "like" a lion. Be on guard! The devil walks around, roaring and pretending to be a lion. The key word here is "like." He is not a lion, but he has learned to roar like one. He'll say or do anything to get you to give up before you even try.

Forever keep this in mind: the devil is a liar. If he can convince you that he is a lion, then he will strip you of your faith in your authority. He will seize the opportunity to enslave you to a life that robs you of your divine potential in Christ. But don't become distracted by the devil's tactics. Remember, he has already been defeated by Jesus at Calvary. The devil has **NO** power to control you! But he will keep roaring as if he does.

Suppose you and I were getting ready to fight. Then I say to you, "Don't bother getting up or even moving. If you do, I'll use this gun, which is right here in my pocket—and that will be the last move you ever make." Now, you might be bigger than I am and have many advantages over me. But, if you never get up for fear of what I said I had in my pocket, I've won. You'll never know that there was really nothing in my pocket. I would have defeated you with *your own thinking.*

This is what the adversary does. He uses lies and deceit to prevent you from knowing the truth of who you really are in Christ so that you won't act upon it and defeat him. Even though he has been disarmed by Christ and rendered powerless, he can cause harm to you by keeping you in the darkness and blind to your full potential in God. He can deprive you of your ability to be a blessing to your family and to your loved ones. His principal mission is to keep you from knowing the truth of God's Word and truly realizing who you are, lest you discover it and live a life of glorifying God by subduing and taking dominion over him and his demons.

Jesus said of satan that the truth is not in him at all. (See John 8:44.) This is important to remember. Jesus said the truth shall make you free. (See John 8:32) We should understand that satan's lies enslave us and deprive us of the freedom the truth brings. satan also knows this and does everything to keep us from knowing the truth.

When we know the truth, we are aware of the divine potential that God has placed in us. We know that through Christ, we can do all things, and nothing is impossible to those who believe and trust in the power of God that works inside them.

satan's Tactics

We first see satan's treachery in the Garden of Eden. He lied to Eve about what God said when he told Adam not to eat of the fruit of the Tree of the Knowledge of Good and Evil. satan was attempting to have the man and the woman substitute knowledge from a source other than God. satan told her in Genesis 3:4, *"You will not surely die."* He went on to tell her that she would become godlike. He knew that her thinking would cause her to fall. He was successful with this double-lie tactic, and he continues to use it to this day. Let us learn from his method.

First, he substituted a lie for the truth. *This caused Eve to think incorrectly about God.* He tells Eve that God was lying when He said that she would die if she ate the fruit. This lie is a direct contradiction of God's Word. In other words, he is saying, "Eve, God's Word is not correct. You need not concern yourself with what God says. It is a lie. This is the real truth. You will not die! You have a mind, so use it."

He uses this same tactic on us today. He gets us to believe that what God says is not true or doesn't apply to us, so we may feel safe in dismissing it. He then manipulates us into believing there is another way *(the substitute)* other than what God says.

It is truly unfortunate that so many people have been led by satan to discount the Word of God. Failing to put the proper value on it, they simply ignore it as though it does not exist. Yet God has told us that His Word is life; we live by it! For this reason masses of people have determined in their hearts to go in a way that is contrary to the will of God. They have been blinded from the truth and then they are led peacefully and ignorantly to destruction. Many will never recognize the error of their ways until it is too late.

Second, he substitutes an inferior identity for our real identity.

This caused Eve to think incorrectly about herself. satan defined an identity for Eve that was inferior to the one God had defined for her. He says, *"Ye shall be as gods, knowing good and evil"* (Genesis 3:5b, KJV). Although God created man in His image, this did *not* make him God or give him the right to try to be God. But just as satan himself wanted to be God and was cast down, he tried to get Eve to put herself in the position of God and suffer the consequences of her rebellion and disobedience to God.

There is nothing new under the sun, and satan continues his same method to this day. He challenges the authenticity of God's Word in your life and seeks to give you a vision of yourself that is not within the will of God. These two tactics are at the root of every attack that he makes against you, because if he is successful, he can distort your thinking.

The Bible says that as a person thinks in his heart, so is he or she. Therefore, if I think on a lie about God's truth, I ultimately distrust God's Word. Or, if I think on a lie about who I am, I believe the lie. The only thing that can set my life straight is the truth of God's Word.

When your thinking is flawed, your actions correspond to your flawed thinking and produce flawed results. Consider Eve: she thought that if she ate the fruit from the Tree of the Knowledge of Good and Evil, it would be good for her. She accepted what satan told her. She also thought she would be like God. Her thinking was wrong and it caused her to sin. Her sinning ultimately and immediately invoked the judgment of a righteous and holy God. It all began with erroneous thinking. Your thinking affects your choices and your choices affect the outcome of your life.

On the other hand, when your thinking is on righteousness, you make righteous choices and thereby you do right. Righteous thinking produces righteous fruit, with the seed to reproduce more and more righteousness that will invoke showers of blessings of God on your life.

satan has many allies in the world to challenge God's Word and affect your thinking. He gets plenty of help from our culture, the media, other people, and our own experiences that lead to wrong thinking and make sure we lead inferior lives. All these things work together to cause us to stumble.

Now hear this!

Your potential is not based upon what others say about you, but it is based totally on what God says about you. Let Him be the author and finisher of your life. Listen and learn His Word and put Him as the architect and general contractor of your life. Don't let satan lie to you about God's Word or tell you that you are someone other than the person God says you are.

The best defense against satan's attacks is to know and be certain of God's will for your life. Know your endless empowerment and your divine directives. Be a reflection of His image. Be blessed and fruitful, multiply, replenish, subdue, and take dominion over the earth. Whenever you encounter an argument that is opposed to all that you know to be true of God's ways, attack and demolish it. Utterly destroy it so that it can't take root in your mind. We have been given this instruction:

> *We demolish arguments and every pretension that sets itself up against the knowledge of God, and we take captive every thought to make it obedient to Christ* (2 Corinthians 10:5).

satan's Tactics and Your Defense

satan doesn't want you to know who you really are. He will come at you when you are weak, vulnerable, and in a mess. When things seem to be going from bad to worse, he'll use your trials to make you doubt who you really are. He'll try to cause you to react in a manner that will hinder the power of God from working in your life.

Remember how he even tried Jesus. After fasting forty days and nights, Jesus was famished and weak. The devil questioned Him with a statement to make Him question His identity and act unbecoming of it, "*If you are the Son of God, tell these stones to become bread*" (Matthew 4:1-3). But Jesus didn't fall for it. He had spent thirty years in preparation, learning who He truly was. Observe how He responded:

> *Jesus answered, "It is written: 'Man does not live on bread alone, but on every word that comes from the mouth of God'*" (Matthew 4:4).

Jesus spoke the Word of God, taking dominion over His flesh, even though He was hungry, and had submitted himself to the Father's will. He did not submit to the tactics of satan. Learn from Jesus. He defeated satan by the Word of God. As Christ did, you must become strong in the Word of God and speak it with authority. Here is what the Bible says about it:

> *Take the helmet of salvation and the **sword of the Spirit, which is the Word of God*** (Ephesians 6:17, emphasis mine).

> ***For the Word of God is living and active. Sharper than any double-edged sword,*** *it penetrates even to dividing soul and spirit, joints and marrow; it judges the thoughts and attitudes of the heart* (Hebrews 4:12, emphasis mine).

You may be thinking, "I can never accomplish that. How can I ever learn to quote the Word back to the enemy?" You can. In fact, you will. Read, meditate, and learn God's Word. In due time, you will confidently take dominion over the devil whenever he comes to tempt you.

Read on in Matthew 4. The devil didn't give up after the first try. Next he takes Jesus to "*the highest point of the temple.*" Then the devil tries to trip Jesus up by misusing the scripture.

Again, the devil starts out with, "*If you are the Son of God, throw yourself down*" (Matthew 4:6). What the devil is really saying is, "You really don't know if you are the Son of God. Come on,

Jesus, *prove* it! If you are who you think you are, you can jump off and not be harmed."

The devil now supposedly quotes scripture.: "God has said, '*He will command angels for you and you will not be hurt.*'" In effect, the challenge from the devil was, "By doing this, there will be no question who you are; you will prove you are the Son of God. You will prove the Word of God is true." The devil does this with a device he commonly uses: misquoting scripture. This time he leaves out a portion of the original scripture that is found in Psalm 91:11.

> *Jesus answered him, "It is also written: 'Do not put the Lord your God to the test'"* (Matthew 4:7).

Jesus understood and again spoke only the Word of God. Then the devil tried a third and final time. He took Jesus "*to a very high mountain and showed him all the kingdoms of the world and their splendor*" (Matthew 4:8). The devil then offered Jesus all worldly riches and power. All Jesus had to do was bow down and worship him.

Satan wanted to be worshiped; this was the real crux of the matter. He wanted to be God. He was the lord of the kingdoms of the world, but these things have no eternal value and Jesus knew this. Therefore, Jesus responded forcefully to satan this time.

> *Jesus said to him, "Away from me, Satan! For it is written: 'Worship the Lord your God, and serve him only'"* (Matthew 4:10).

"*Then the devil left him, and angels came and attended him*" (Matthew 4:11). There is nothing in this world of more value than the eternal blessing of worshiping and serving the Lord our God.

Jesus rejected satan's encouraging offers each time by quoting God's Word. You also must never substitute anything for what God says for your life. No matter what the circumstances seem to indicate, speak what God says about His will for your life. Declare it and stand on it!

- Hang in there and keep pressing into the Word of God and studying it. Remember that God is working with you so you will be successful at knowing it.
- Keep believing and speaking the Word of God. Remember, it was His Word that created the universe, and the universe will respond to His Word.
- Wait on the Lord and be of good courage. He will not forsake you or forget you.
- Be patient, and the angels will come and attend to you after you too have been proven faithful.

You too will be tempted by the devil just like Jesus was. In like manner, satan will try to trick you into disobeying God or try to persuade you to prove your identity by ungodly means. He might tempt you to show off your kingship, scare you into a corner, and try to get you to put God to the test. By subtle means, he will see if you'll step out of line and deviate from your true character. He might even offer you worldly riches and power if only you'll bow down and serve him. Remember, you're the one with the authority. Use it! You easily overcome him with the Word of God.

Remember 1 Peter 5:8: "*Be self-controlled and alert. Your enemy the devil prowls around like a roaring lion looking for someone to devour.*"

Know God's Word before satan attacks. Find and **Meditate, Apply, and Perform** God's Word so that you know His will for your life. **MAP!** it. Use your Bible. Don't just read it; study it. If there's an issue in your life and you're not sure about it, look it up. There is nothing new under the sun. God has already dealt with any situation that you encounter.

> "*For I know the plans I have for you,*" declares the Lord, "*plans to prosper you and not to harm you, plans to give you hope and a future*" (Jeremiah 29:11).

He has plans to prosper you and give you hope, but what good are those plans if you don't know them and align yourself with His will for you? Lack of knowledge will hinder your prosperity and prevent you from achieving your divine potential.

Additionally, listen to good preaching and reject preaching that is not in line with the Word of God. Remove yourself from people and churches that are not in line with God's Word. Fellowship with people of a like mind at church, at work, and at play.

Be careful about what you feed yourself: the things you see on TV or listen to on the radio or read in magazines. Don't let anybody or anything sway you from believing in God's Word. Your life depends on it! *"They are not just idle words for you—they are your life. By them you will live long in the land you are crossing the Jordan to possess"* (Deuteronomy 32:47).

When you find scriptures that speak to you personally, keep them before you. Put them on your refrigerator, on your mirror, on your visor, on your screen saver. Feast upon them. Get drunk on them. Remember God will honor His Word. When you find it, hold onto it and hold Him to it!

Now, when the devil comes at you with roaring lies, how will you respond?

- You're poor and will always be poor; there is no way for you to get ahead.
- Satan will take your children. They will be on drugs, in gangs, and living for him.
- You're slow; you'll never make good grades.
- God's Word does not work for you.
- You're sick and going to die.
- If you do things the way the world does, you'll be successful and get the things you desire.
- No one knows what you've been through; no one understands.
- If you really were a child of God, this would not be happening to you.
- Your spouse is going to be late tonight because he/she is with another (woman or man).

Understand that satan is going to come after you. If he tempted Jesus, he is most certainly going to tempt you. Don't discuss what he says to you with him (as Eve did). Don't negotiate for even one second; instead, use the Word as the final authority and respond (like Christ) with the Word of God, which is your sword. Don't keep your weapon in your pocket. Pull it out and use it! You are God's property. The devil has no authority over you, except what you give him. Therefore, do not negotiate, do not compromise. Answer the devil without hesitation.

When the devil roars at you, USE YOUR WEAPON.

- You're poor and will always be poor; there is no way for you to get ahead.
    - God will give me the ability to acquire wealth.
- satan will take your children. They will be on drugs, in gangs, and living for him.
    - God will form a hedge of protection around me and my family, and no weapon formed against us shall prosper.
- You're slow; you'll never make good grades.
    - I have the mind of Christ, and I can do all things through Christ who strengthens me.
- God's Word does not work for you.
    - God's Word will not return to Him void. He is watching to see that it accomplishes what He sent it to do.
- You're sick and you're going to die.
    - God sent His Word to heal others and He will come to my sickbed and I shall recover.
- If you do things the way the world does, you'll be successful and get the many things you desire.
    - There is a way that seems right to a man, but in the end, the way is death. I shall choose the way of God.
- No one knows what you've been through; no one understands.
    - Jesus was a man despised and rejected by men. He was a man of sorrows and familiar with suffering.

> He understands what I'm going through, and He
> will not allow any more to come upon me than what
> I can bear.

- If you really were a child of God, this would not be happening to you.
  - The rain falls on the just as well as the unjust and in this world, you will have trouble, but I take heart because Jesus has overcome the world for me.
- Your spouse is going to be late tonight because he/she is with another (woman or man).
  - I have not been given the spirit of fear, but of power and of love and of a sound mind.

Beware the Grasshopper Mentality!

All that the world has taught you to believe about yourself will keep you enslaved to an inferior life. God created you, and He alone has the right to tell you who you are. Knowing who you are influences how you will respond to any situation.

Do you remember the behavior of the Israelites when Moses was able to get their freedom from Pharaoh? The Lord had said to Moses:

> *Then say to Pharaoh, "This is what the Lord says: Israel is my firstborn son, and I told you, 'Let my son go, so he may worship me.' But you refused to let him go; so I will kill your firstborn son"* (Exodus 4:22-23).

They had all heard that they were God's firstborn son. They saw all of the miracles that were performed for them to obtain their freedom. They indeed saw the death of the firstborn of all the Egyptians and the pillar of cloud to lead them by day and the pillar of fire to give them light that they might travel by night. Yet, when Pharaoh came after them at the Red Sea, they completely forgot they were the firstborn of God. They were willing to go back to Egypt as slaves rather than trust God to lead them to freedom as His children. They did not understand who they truly were!

Even Moses didn't realize the complete authority that had been given to him. The Lord said to him, because of the authority he had within him, "*Why are you crying out to me? Tell the Israelites to move on. Raise your staff and stretch out your hand over the sea to divide the water so that the Israelites can go through the sea on dry ground*" (Exodus 14:15-16). In other words, "Moses, I have given you the authority to lead these people to the Promised Land. Use your authority!" Then God worked through Moses to fulfill His will in the earth. Moses needed to remember who he was and the people needed to remember who they were. What needless grief they all went through because they did not accept who God said they were.

When Moses lifted up his hand over the sea, the supernatural occurred. A strong east wind held the sea back all night and made the seabed dry land. The waters were divided so the people could cross. Then, when Moses lifted up his hand over the sea the second time, it returned to its normal course and all of the Egyptians that had followed the Israelites were drowned. The people saw it all.

A short time later the people again failed to realize who they truly were and once again doubted the Word of the Lord. Numbers 13 explains how Moses sent a leader from each tribe of Israel to scout out the land promised to them by God. The leaders were strong, wise, confident, and sure-footed men who were respected and honored. They had already been tested and proven. But they had not learned to see themselves as children of God, nor had they learned to trust the Word of God. When they returned, they reported a beautiful land flowing with milk and honey, like the Lord promised, but then they declared:

- The people are powerful and stronger than we are.
- The cities are very big and fortified.
- There are giants in the land.

A most revealing statement is found in Numbers 13:33 when the leaders reported, "*We saw the Nephilim there ... We seemed like grasshoppers in our own eyes, and we looked the same to them.*" Here we learn that the way you learn to see yourself influences the way other people see you. You must learn to see yourself as God sees you and not be moved by what you see with your eyes. You must learn to walk by faith and not by sight.

- They saw things from their perspective.
- They were affected by their physical circumstances.
- They did not recognize God in their reality.
- They thought of themselves as grasshoppers.
- Because they thought of themselves as grasshoppers, the enemy did also.
- They were defeated before they even tried to win.

Out of all these leaders, only Joshua and Caleb had confidence that the Lord would give this Promised Land to them. Yes, it is true that in the natural, all that was reported was factual. Even so, Joshua and Caleb knew that if the Lord was with them, there was nothing to be afraid of! There was nothing too big for their God! Unfortunately, the scripture continues to report that the people chose to believe the word of their leaders rather than trust the Word of God.

> *That night all the people of the community raised their voices and wept aloud. All the Israelites grumbled against Moses and Aaron, and the whole assembly said to them, "If only we had died in Egypt! Or in this desert! Why is the Lord bringing us to this land only to let us fall by the sword? Our wives and children will be taken as plunder. Wouldn't it be better for us to go back to Egypt?" And they said to each other, "We should choose a leader and go back to Egypt"* (Numbers 14:1-4).

Clearly, negative thinking causes negative actions. Although there were possibly a million people in the camp, "a little leaven spoils the whole loaf." The lesson for you is to isolate yourself from negative-thinking people.

The Israelites' failure to realize the power they had was devastatingly ruinous. God said:

> *The Lord said to Moses and Aaron: "How long will this wicked community grumble against me? I have heard the*

complaints of these grumbling Israelites. So tell them, 'As surely as I live, declares the Lord, I will do to you the very things I heard you say: In this desert your bodies will fall— every one of you twenty years old or more who was counted in the census and who has grumbled against me. Not one of you will enter the land I swore with uplifted hand to make your home, except Caleb son of Jephunneh and Joshua son of Nun. As for your children that you said would be taken as plunder, I will bring them in to enjoy the land you have rejected. But you—your bodies will fall in this desert. Your children will be shepherds here for forty years, suffering for your unfaithfulness, until the last of your bodies lies in the desert. For forty years—one year for each of the forty days you explored the land—you will suffer for your sins and know what it is like to have me against you.' I, the Lord, have spoken, and I will surely do these things to this whole wicked community, which has banded together against me. They will meet their end in this desert; here they will die" (Numbers 14: 26-35).

The Promised Land waited for a new generation who could believe in God, while those who doubted died out. Just as Joshua and Caleb did, we must trust what God has said about us and be willing to deal with the things of the world that come against us. Only then may we enter into the abundant life that God has promised to us. God gives us time to learn, then He expects us to act upon that knowledge and live our lives for His glory. It is now time to find out who God says you are!

God said, "*Let us make man in our image.*" (See Genesis 1:26.)

Therefore ...
God determined your course in life.
    Your race, the color of your skin, your gender, and your social status do not determine your course in life. GOD DOES! If you don't listen to Him and allow His Word to define who you are, you subject yourself to being pressured to be what the world and others

view you to be. Allowing others to be your gods, defining your life and negatively influencing you, is not God's will for your life!

Remember these great men of God:

- God showed Joseph his destiny in dreams. Joseph maintained the faith and the Word of God while he was a slave and a prisoner, until he was exalted by Pharaoh to be the second greatest man in the Kingdom of Egypt.

- Moses spent forty years in Pharaoh's court, being what they told him he was, before he knew and accepted who he really was. (See Hebrews 11:24-25.) Then Moses spent forty more years in the wilderness to come to know who God said he was.

- Samson, following the Word of God that was spoken over him as a child, refused to allow his hair to be cut and obeyed the Word of the Lord. He became the strongest man who ever lived.

- Gideon's tribe was the weakest tribe of the nation and Gideon was the least of his family. God called him a mighty man of valor and when Gideon accepted what God told him, God used him to deliver the nation with only 300 men.

- David was a mere shepherd, and he was small in stature. Then God told him who he really was. Resisting persecution and dire circumstances, he became the greatest king of Israel.

- Peter was a quick-tempered, unstable fisherman until he learned who God said he really was. He developed strength and became solid as a rock.

The writer of the Book of Hebrews included some of these men when he spoke of their faith in what God said:

And what more shall I say? I do not have time to tell about Gideon, Barak, Samson, Jephthah, David, Samuel and the prophets, who through faith conquered kingdoms, administered justice, and gained what was promised; who shut the mouths of lions, quenched the fury of the flames, and escaped the edge of the sword; whose weakness was turned to strength; and who became powerful in battle and routed foreign armies (Hebrews 11:32-34).

History and the Bible tell us how great each of these men was and how God was able to use them, but not one started out as a person who exhibited unusual potential. They certainly must have seemed ordinary to their countrymen, and likely seemed ordinary to themselves. Society probably had them convinced that they weren't special or worthy of greatness—until God took over. Don't underestimate the pressure of influence that can change you from being godly or keep you from ever realizing your divine potential. Stay away from those who challenge the Word of God in your life.

Until these men found out what God had created them for, their divine potential and their very lives could not be changed. They had to agree and choose. The only way to break the influence of the world and the chains of its bondage is to choose the influence of God. When God told each man his specific mission, each one believed Him and it changed their lives forever. This works the same way in your life.

God said, "Let us make man in our image." (See Genesis 1:26.) Therefore …

You Don't Have to Settle for Second Best!

God created you to be the head and not the tail. Never settle for less than that! God has given you the ability to set things in order and to line things up according to His purpose for your life. The place you are in right now is a result of choices you have made. You set up an order of events to serve your own purpose. And the situations in your life are direct consequences of these choices.

• You chose your relationships.

- You chose to work for your employer.
- You chose your level of integrity.
- You chose the people with whom you associate.
- You chose how you spend your time.

If you have chosen badly, you can re-choose. You can choose to line up with God's purpose for your life. Know who you are. Settle for nothing less than God's best: His plan for you! Start making right choices and your life will turn around. Choose to be who God says you are!

God said, *"Let us make man in our image"* (See Genesis 1:26). **Therefore ...**

You Are Part of the Body of Christ

The world is filled with a variety of people, all created by God with a purpose and differing talents and gifts, different sizes and shapes, and relative strengths and weaknesses; all are meant to work together as one in Christ. But due to division, perceived superiority and inferiority, and corruption, some have chosen not to work as one in the Body of Christ.

The devil wants you to focus on things other than your divine potential. Consequently he calls your attention to your skin color, outward appearance, strengths, or weaknesses—anything that makes you "different" or separates you from other people. This creates division in the Body. When you focus on differences and separations, you can't operate with the mind of Christ. No, if you think you're inferior, you're racked by insecurity. If you think you're superior, you're self-important and arrogant.

If you forget that you were created in God's image for a specific purpose, you will also forget that you are not of this world. You'll lose your true identity and become weak. Ultimately, you will become defeated. You'll live an inferior life-style that will be imposed upon you, even if it seems to have all the trappings of prestige and superiority. If the life you choose is not in line with God's will, you're not living the abundant life.

But once you get the Word richly dwelling in you and take on the true image of God, even if the earth shakes and trembles, you will not fall.

God said, *"Let us make man in our image." (See Genesis 1:26).* Therefore ...
You are made of clay, so let God shape you into what He knows best!

> *The Lord God formed man from the dust of the ground* (Genesis 2:7).

> *Yet, O LORD, you are our Father. We are the clay, you are the potter; we are all the work of your hand* (Isaiah 64:8),

God is your loving Father; you can trust Him with your very life. You are sensitive to His touch and allow Him to mold and fashion you into His image.

> *But we have this treasure in jars of clay to show that this all-surpassing power is from God and not from us. We are hard pressed on every side, but not crushed; perplexed, but not in despair; persecuted, but not abandoned; struck down, but not destroyed* (2 Corinthians 4:7-9).

God wants you to achieve your divine potential so that His surpassing power within you will shine out through you. It is God's pleasure to work with you to make you an overcomer. The weaker you think you are, the softer you become and the easier it is for God to mold you into what He wants you to be. Remember, you are the clay that God sculpts into a vessel of honor to show that the power to succeed is from Him.

When you are being *"hard pressed on every side,"* remember you will not be crushed as long as you are yielding to God. No matter what you are going through, God's strength will be perfected through your weakness. And when you obtain the victory over your trial, everyone will know God did it. The more you yield to His will, the more He shapes you.

Outwardly you may appear to be wearing down, but inwardly you are being renewed everyday. It may not feel like it now, but this will only last for a moment. When you keep your focus on Jesus, you tap into a peace that goes beyond all your natural reasoning.

Romans 12:2 (NKJV) instructs, *"And do not be conformed to this world, but be transformed by the renewing of your mind."* The transformation process will be automatic when your mind is renewed. This Scripture empowers you to choose.

You can choose to go with your own purpose
Or
You can make the right choices and choose God's purpose for you.

Now is the time to:

- Stop conforming to the world around you.
- Stop listening to the world's way of doing things.
- Stop letting the world be your potter.
- Stop being influenced by others.
- Go to God and let His will rule.
- Go to the Word and let your mind be transformed.
- Go to prayer and let God speak His purpose into your life.
- Go to listen to the Master Sculptor, your heavenly Father, and let Him shape and mold you into His image.

Breaking the Bondage of the Past
Have you ever noticed a full-grown elephant that is bound by a tiny stake in the ground? It would take little effort for this huge creature to break loose and experience freedom, but he never makes the effort. Why?

When an elephant is a baby, he is fastened to a spike. He's not strong enough to break free. All of the baby elephant's tugging, twisting, and turning fail. Based on his experience, he concludes that he's weak. His reality (not reality at all) is set for life. Therefore, later, when he could easily jerk up the stake and walk away, this great beast won't even try. He has given up and submitted to captivity.

This full-grown, powerful elephant is living in the past. As a result, he doesn't seize his potential. He doesn't use His God-given strength and natural abilities. He doesn't even realize his enormous size. Instead, he locks himself into his past experiences of failure and inadequacy. Maybe that is why it's said that an elephant never forgets.

The Israelites were like this. They were in bondage to Egypt for 400 years. Generations lived and died. Babies were born conditioned to oppression. This life-style, like that of the captive elephant, became all they knew. They accepted it as a way of life.

Even as God was delivering them, they struggled with disbelief and discouragement. They experienced feelings of inadequacy and even wanted to be left alone and return to serve the Egyptians.

Some Christians are still living in Egypt; they have been set free but don't know it:

- They don't know who they are.
- They can't believe God desires great things for them and has given them the potential to achieve.
- They don't study God's Word enough to know the truth about their freedom.
- They have accepted another's word for reality other than accepting what God has to say.

Some Christians are living happily in bondage, and do not want to break free:

- They continuously live in bondage to government-assistance programs.
- They continuously live in bondage to handouts from others.
- They continuously live in bondage to other human beings.
- They continuously live in bondage to sin.
- They continuously live in bondage to financial debt.

115

- They continuously live in bondage to destructive addictions.

Some Christians, even though God speaks against it, find it hard to believe that God can make a way out of:

- Sickness
- Poverty
- Addictions to drugs, sex, gambling, and alcohol
- Child abuse/spouse abuse
- Negative attitudes
- Doubt and unbelief

But this will not be you!

You will shake free from the past, from your old way of doing things, even the way you were trained to think. No form of bondage will hold on to you any longer. You are now in Christ, and you are becoming aware of your divine potential!

Because of who you are in Christ:
- Nothing can keep you down.
- Nothing can keep you bound.
- Nothing can keep you from achieving your divine potential—nothing, that is, but YOU!

Because of who you are in Christ, God will deliver you from your bondage, no matter what it is. It's time to take the shackles off your mind.

God said, "*Let us make man in our image.*" (See Genesis 1:26.) Therefore ...

You Are a Child of God.

Because you have a divine potential invested in you by God, you're no longer of this world. Your *"citizenship is in heaven"* (Philippians 3:20). You are a child of God who was created to worship

Him. As His child, you are under His protection and care. He won't allow anything to keep you in bondage or harm you. By looking to your heavenly Father for deliverance, you can see His mighty hand and outstretched arm working in your life. The supernatural will occur for you because you are His child and He is your Father. He is no respecter of persons; what He has done for others, He will do for you.

> *Therefore, say to the Israelites: "I am the LORD, and I will bring you out from under the yoke of the Egyptians. I will free you from being slaves to them, and I will redeem you with an outstretched arm and with mighty acts of judgment. I will take you as my own people, and I will be your God. Then you will know that I am the LORD your God, who brought you out from under the yoke of the Egyptians"* (Exodus 6:6-7).

Remember the Hebrews living with the Egyptians in Pharaoh's land. When God sent His judgment, chaos broke out only over Egypt, but it didn't touch the Hebrews because they were God's children. You can expect this same protection from the chaos of the world. God is still the same today. He will protect you from all harm.

> *Surely he will save you from the fowler's snare and from the deadly pestilence. He will cover you with his feathers, and under his wings you will find refuge; his faithfulness will be your shield and rampart. You will not fear the terror of night, nor the arrow that flies by day, nor the pestilence that stalks in the darkness, nor the plague that destroys at midday. A thousand may fall at your side, ten thousand at your right hand, but it will not come near you* (Psalm 91: 3-7).

As God's child, you can:

- approach Him.
- receive from Him.
- communicate with Him.

- worship Him.
- trust Him; God will make a way, even when you can see no way.

As a born-again child of God, you are a new creature in Christ. The old things have passed away and all things are new. God has given you a new spirit; when you enter into an intimate relationship with Him, you enter into an impending state of metamorphosis. Your intimacy with Him interlocks the new spirit He has given you with His Spirit. The resulting union of the Spirit of God with your spirit gives birth to a new person whose spiritual DNA is part human and part divine. On the outside, it might not look like much is happening, but on the inside, you're changing and becoming more like Christ.

The more you meditate on the Word of God and fellowship with God, the more your life transforms. The more you attend a true Bible-teaching church, study the Word, and fellowship with other like-minded Christians, the easier the metamorphosis is. As your life transforms, you experience what is good and pleasing, moving closer and closer to the perfect will of God for your life. (See Romans 12:2.) Before you even realize it, the ways of the world are no longer your ways at all. You think differently, see things in a different light, and respond differently to the challenges in your life. You experience the reality of the empowerment of God to such an extent that the promises of God are manifest in your life in increasing measure.

When the appointed time comes, you stretch your wings, mount up, and soar above your problems. The things that used to keep you bound will bind you no more!

> *But they that wait upon [trust in] the LORD shall renew their strength; they shall mount up with wings as eagles; they shall run, and not be weary; and they shall walk, and not faint* (Isaiah 40:31).

You need the Word of God planted in your heart and mind, so place yourself in a church and around other believers, where you may feed on the Word. To truly clean up your life, fill it daily with

God's Word to accomplish all that He intends. It will not fail or fall short. It will take some time, but His Word's effect on your life is certain to accomplish much.

Remember that transformation doesn't happen overnight; it is progressive. The devil will push and hurry you along to do things his way. God will, however, lead you gently, patiently, and kindly to the place where He wants you to go.

I once tried to get God to hurry up and do something with my life. I was twenty-six years old when I told Him, "You had better hurry up and do something with me, God. I am getting old."

He answered, "Who are you to talk about how old you are? If I want you to live to be 101 years old before you fulfill my purpose, it will be so."

It's very human to sense a feeling of urgency when you're on a task or a mission—especially one that you think has a deadline. We live in a culture that drives us to instant gratification, multi-tasking, and quick fixes. We're always in a hurry. So how do you handle a sense of urgency? Remember always that God ultimately controls our time. He's always the final authority over what, when, where, and how. So, don't rush into anything. Wait on the Lord! Make sure you're working with Him, so His purpose will be fulfilled.

God controls time and He never has to force anything. But satan will, just to get you to make mistakes. Remember this: if God is with you, satan can't stop you. And since satan can't stop you, he will try to push you and get you into a rush that will cause you to get ahead of God's timing. Urgency is not of God. Be patient and allow God to perfect you. At the right time, you will be allowed to triumph.

God said, *"Let us make man in our image."* (See Genesis 1:26). Therefore ...

You Are a Friend of God.

You've got a friend who is so close that all you have to say is "Jesus," and He is right there with you. Unlike other friends we have known, Jesus never leaves you alone or turns His back on you. When you feel alone, He is there with you. In the midnight hour, when your tears have soaked your pillow and it seems that no one else cares, He comes to comfort you. He dries your weeping eyes. He longs for you to be as close to Him as He is to you.

When you're aware of Jesus' friendship, you act like a friend of His. You walk and talk with Him. You discover His likes and dislikes. As you learn more about Him and His love for you, you fall in love with Him. Reverence for Him comes more easily at this stage. You seek God's presence with your whole heart, mind, and soul.

Jesus explained how His friendship with the Father allowed him to do what the Father did:

> *I tell you the truth, the Son can do nothing by himself; he can do only what he sees his Father doing, because whatever the Father does the Son also does. For the Father loves the Son and shows him all he does. Yes, to your amazement he will show him even greater things than these* (John 5:19-20).

Jesus did what He saw His Father do. Just as a young child will mimic his parents, so does a child of God imitate what he or she sees his or her father doing. How are you to become aware of what the Father does? You spend time communicating with Him. You become His friend, as Jesus said above.

The Greek word for "love" in this verse is *Phileo,* which means. "is friends with." Therefore, we can read it this way: "For the Father is friends with the Son, and shows Him all He does." Because Jesus was friends with the Father, the Father allowed Him to see things that He could do.

When you make yourself God's friend, conduct your life in a manner that is both right and just, and teach your family to do the same, then God will keep no secrets from you. In fact, He will reveal to you great and wonderful things you never knew (See Jeremiah 33:3), including His will for you.

Listen to how God talked with Abraham, his friend, near the trees at Mamre:

> *When the men got up to leave, they looked down toward Sodom, and Abraham walked along with them to see them on their way. Then the LORD said, "Shall I hide from Abraham*

what I am about to do? Abraham will surely become a great and powerful nation, and all nations on earth will be blessed through him. For I have chosen him, so that he will direct his children and his household after him to keep the way of the LORD by doing what is right and just, so that the LORD will bring about for Abraham what he has promised him" (Genesis 18:16-19).

As you read about Abraham in James 2:23, you learn that it pleases God when you believe in Him and in His Word: *"And the scripture was fulfilled that says, 'Abraham believed God, and it was credited to him as righteousness,' **and he was called God's friend"*** (emphasis mine). God counts your belief as your righteousness, and calls you His friend—all this just because you believe, trust, and have faith in Him.

God said, *"Let us make man in our image."* (See Genesis 1:26). **Therefore ...**

You Are Spiritually Minded.

Repent and be baptized, every one of you, in the name of Jesus Christ for the forgiveness of your sins. And you will receive the gift of the Holy Spirit (Acts 2:38).

Something dynamic happens to you when you let go of sin and choose to follow Jesus Christ. You receive the Holy Spirit, become spiritually minded, and operate in a realm that is not influenced by the natural. You think outside the realm of the world system. You start to look at things from an entirely different perspective. Instead of reviewing life through your five natural senses, you develop a sixth sense to see things in the spirit and command the power thereof as you walk after the Spirit.

Together with God, your divine potential gives you the ability to connect with the Holy Spirit who has no limitations. With the Holy Spirit:

- You can drive out demons. (See Matthew 12:28.)
- You can speak life and have life. (See John 6:63.)
- You can speak by the Spirit. (See Matthew 22:43.)
- You can be full of joy. (See John 15:11.)
- You do the impossible. (See John 14:12.)
- You can enter into all truth. (See John 16:13.)
- You know what is yet to come. (See John 16:13.)
- You prophesy, see visions, and dream dreams. (See Acts 2:17.)
- You speak the Word of God boldly. (See Acts 4:31.)
- You are full of the Spirit and wisdom. (See Acts 6:3.)

Being spiritually minded, you have a new sense of boldness and power in your life. You have a new confidence and peace that come from knowing that God is backing up His plan for you! You step out of the ways and thoughts that are NOT the real you, and you step into who you really are. You are less concerned about what you see with your physical eyes and are more focused on what you see with your spiritual eyes. Through the Spirit, you enter a place that pleases God—a place where miracles happen!

This is where God wants you to be in fellowship with His Spirit. This is where your divine-potential power is truly manifest. For God has said, " ... *not by might, nor by power, but by my Spirit*" (Zechariah 4:6). Jesus said to His own disciples, *"But you will receive power when the Holy Spirit comes on you; and you will be my witnesses in Jerusalem, and in all Judea and Samaria, and to the ends of the earth"* (Acts 1: 8).

The power of the Lord awaits you. It's time to seize your divine potential! It's yours!

DIVINE POTENTIAL POWER POINTS

Do You Know Who You Are?

1) God Determines Your Course in Life.

2) You Don't Have to Settle for Second Best.

3) You Are Part of the Body of Christ. You are created to function in the Church. You are meant to be a vital part of the Body of Christ, fulfilling an even greater corporate potential.

4) You Are Clay. It's your choice to let God or the world mold you.

5) You Are a Child of God. God promises His children supernatural deliverance and the ability to soar above all bondage.

6) You Are a Friend of God. God will never turn His back on you.

7) You Are Spiritually Minded. You can see, listen to, speak, and do the impossible.

When you focus on the Almighty God and His promises for you, impossibilities become possible! You are empowered by God to seize your divine potential. Rise up and take hold of it!

My Divine Potential Prayer for You!

I pray you will find your place in the Body of Christ and discover your God-given giftings and abilities—all helping you to grow in faith and wisdom. I pray the Holy Spirit will mold and fashion you into a vessel of honor.

I pray you will be set free from all bondage in your life. I pray that God will deliver you from all evil and fill you to overflowing with His presence—with His joy, and that He will teach you how to let go and be free in Him.

I pray you will see yourself in your new image—not in the natural, but in the Spirit. I pray that the Holy Spirit will teach you how to be a faithful friend of God, will lead you to places that only He can, and will help you to achieve greatness. In Jesus' name I pray. Amen.

CHAPTER 6

Performance Principle Number Two

Align Yourself With the Word of God

Facing Natural Reality

We have already talked about finding out who you are in the Word of God. Now it is time to check yourself to see how you line up with what God says. As you come to know who you really are, you will recognize areas in your life that don't fit with the truth of God's Word. Don't be afraid or discouraged. Instead, recognize those uneasy moments as evidence that you're changing, and set your mind upon aligning yourself with God. You're going to be amazed at the results!

God's Blessing and His Divine Potential Are Conditional

All that God is offering you is guaranteed to you only if you are faithful to Him and seek to keep His Word. Let us consider a scripture that supports this:

> *If anyone loves me, he will obey my teaching. My Father will love him, and we will come to him and make our home with him* (John 14:23).

I would like to reveal another point to you. Do you remember when satan tempted Jesus by having Him stand on the highest point of the Temple? Remember how he referred to Psalms 91 when he told Jesus to throw himself down? He was revealing that he knows the scripture and can quote from it. Just because satan knows the Word very well, does this mean that he has great faith? Or does it suggest that he has the presence of God with him? *No!*

Now, what's the difference between the devil who knows the Word and people who attend church and know the Word very well? Unfortunately in many cases, there is little or no difference. The devil and his demons may know the Word, but they don't do the Word. In order to be anointed with the presence of God, you must do more than just find the Word of God; you must align yourself with it. You must be a doer of the Word. When you are in action in the Word, Jesus says that He and His father will come and make their home with you. I give you another scripture:

> *For whoever does the will of my Father in heaven is my brother and sister and mother* (Matthew 12:50).

When we do the Word of God, Jesus says that we prove we are of the family of God. And if we are the family of God, we have the ability to do as a child of God would do. What did Jesus do? He did the will of the Father and did great works. What does that mean for you? When you do the will of the Father (are aligned with it), you too will do great works—and even greater works, because God will assist you in achieving your divine potential. The key is finding and doing what the Word of God says.

Eliminating Sin

Sin separates us from God. It keeps us from achieving our divine potential. Therefore, we must align ourselves with God's Word at all times.

> *If I had cherished sin in my heart, the Lord would not have listened* (Psalm 66:18).

> *Surely the arm of the Lord is not too short to save, nor his ear too dull to hear. But your iniquities have separated you*

from your God; your sins have hidden his face from you, so that he will not hear (Isaiah 59:1-2).

When you correct those things in your life that are contrary to God's Word, blessings chase you down and run you over. For example, you can read in Luke 15:11-24 about the prodigal son who did not use godly wisdom and did things according to his own will. As a result, he entered a tragic cycle that was not broken until he acknowledged that he was not in the will of his father and set his will to correct his error. You must be willing to do this too.

God had a plan for the prodigal son's future (just as He has a plan for yours). However, the son chose to go a different way. He asked his father for his inheritance, and then *"set off for a distant country and there squandered his wealth in wild living"* (Luke 15:13). He reaped what he sowed. Then, "a severe famine" devastated this distant country. In need of a job, the Prodigal Son fed pigs for a living. The income from the job was so poor that *"He longed to fill his stomach with the pods that the pigs were eating, but no one gave him anything"* (Luke 15:16).

Finally, the prodigal son took a hard look at his situation and faced the truth that he was in this position because of his own bad decisions. He realized how senseless his life had been. He then remembered his father's house and how the many *"hired men have food to spare,"* while here he was "starving to death!" The Bible says, *"He came to his senses"* (Luke 15:17). He faced the fact that he was not aligned with his father's wishes.

The prodigal son then **visualized** (created a mental image) regarding how he would return to his father's house and make things right. Then he **verbalized**: *"I will set out and go back to my father and say to him: Father, I have sinned against heaven and against you. I am no longer worthy to be called your son; make me like one of your hired men"* (Luke 15:18).

If you take a close look at it, you see the acronym of faith that I mentioned earlier. He knew his father's will was not for him to be in the condition he was in. He was out of order with his father's will, but he was willing to take steps to become in alignment with it. When he verbalized, he said, "I'll ask my father to make me like one of his hired men." Then he took action and returned home to his father.

Here is where you witness one of the deepest forms of love—the love of a father for his son, the unconditional love that the heavenly Father has for you. The once- prodigal son then entered into a true relationship with his father where they spoke heart-to-heart. The son received a new level of blessings and submitted himself to his father's will.

> *But while he was still a long way off, his father saw him and was filled with compassion for him; he ran to his son, threw his arms around him and kissed him. The son said to him, 'Father, I have sinned against heaven and against you. I am no longer worthy to be called your son.' But the father said to his servants, 'Quick! Bring the best robe and put it on him. Put a ring on his finger and sandals on his feet. Bring the fattened calf and kill it. Let's have a feast and celebrate. For this son of mine was dead and is alive again; he was lost and is found.' So they began to celebrate* (Luke 15:20-24).

When the son was willing to return to the father, the father restored him to the position he had lost. This is what our heavenly Father is willing to do with us if we will simply return to Him. Even if we have strayed far, when we get in line with His Word, He is willing to forgive us and to restore us to our divine potential.

If you've been like the prodigal son, it is not too late to restore your relationship with your heavenly Father. Come to your senses and realize that you're disconnected from the Word of God, and then go and make things right. Repent to your heavenly Father.

When you repent, something happens inside of you. At the feet of your heavenly Father, you're healed, renewed, and strengthened to walk in your true calling. You're empowered with a fresh force of energy. This means you're able to discern the good and the bad about yourself. You're ready to start making wrong things right. It's never too late to get started.

Here are just a few scriptures to help you understand the importance of being in line with God's Word. It is very important for you to realize God's blessings are conditional. They are guaranteed only to those who are faithful to Him and seek to honor His Word in their lives.

> *I tell you the truth, anyone who has faith in me will do what I have been doing. He will do even greater things than these, because I am going to the Father. And I will do whatever you ask in my name, so that the Son may bring glory to the Father. You may ask me for anything in my name, and I will do it* (John 14:12-14).

In this scripture, Jesus lets you know that by faith, you will do what He did. He is telling you that there is a potential inside you and that, as your faith is developed, you will be able to accomplish the great works He has done. When you ask for things in His name, He will do them so that the Father may be glorified. It is important to understand you must live your life to glorify God, not to exalt yourself. You will never achieve your divine potential if your purpose is selfish. Your divine potential is available to you for the purpose of being a blessing to others and bringing glory to God.

This next scripture helps us to understand how we may have the presence of God within us. It is His presence that gives us the power to accomplish the impossible. Whether or not you align with God is your choice alone.

> *If you remain in me and my words remain in you, ask whatever you wish, and it will be given you. This is to my Father's glory, that you bear much fruit, showing yourselves to be my disciples. As the Father has loved me, so have I loved you. Now remain in my love. If you obey my commands, you will remain in my love, just as I have obeyed my Father's commands and remain in his love. I have told you this so that my joy may be in you and that your joy may be complete* (John 15:7-11).

You are required to be aligned with God's Word. When you are aligned with God's Word, your joy will be complete and you'll be able to accomplish the "impossible."

Finally, this next Scripture discusses alignment and agreement with the will of God for your life. It's tremendously exciting that God will keep His covenant with you.

> *If you pay attention to these laws and are careful to follow them, then the Lord your God will keep his covenant of love with you, as he swore to your forefathers. He will love you and bless you and increase your numbers. He will bless the fruit of your womb, the crops of your land—your grain, new wine and oil—the calves of your herds and the lambs of your flocks in the land that he swore to your forefathers to give you. You will be blessed more than any other people; none of your men or women will be childless, nor any of your livestock without young. The Lord will keep you free from every disease. He will not inflict on you the horrible diseases you knew in Egypt, but he will inflict them on all who hate you* (Deuteronomy 7:12-15).

In summary, the scriptures reveal that nothing is promised unless His Word remains in us and we are obedient to it. If you are now receiving what you believe to be blessings and yet are not aligned with His Word, you have not received the fullness of what God has promised. You're merely receiving crumbs from the table—the leftovers. The complete food is for the faithful who will do His will. Think of how wonderfully blessed you will be when you are simply obedient to the Word.

Know this: no one can serve two masters. Through your actions, you are either serving God or satan, and you will receive wages from your master. If you are serving God, He will sign your check with blessings. If you are serving satan, he will sign your check with death. To receive from God, you must know God's Word. You must **find it** and then you must **align** yourself with it. It must remain in you. It must be a part of you. Eat, live, sleep, and drink His Word so that you will be careful to obey it.

God will always honor His Word. He will do what He says He will do. The only condition is that you must be **aligned** with it.

To illustrate, let's imagine that you have a job where your boss agrees to pay you $300 a week. You work for three weeks and find out that your boss is a generous and loving person. However, in spite of a fair wage and a good boss, you decide to quit. You go to your boss and inform him that you won't be working anymore, but would still like to receive your salary. He, of course, sees no reason to continue paying you and refuses. This is the same way life works with God. If you won't do what He asks of you, you cannot expect to receive His blessings.

There are two steps you need to take to get aligned with God's Word:

Step #1 – See things as they are.
Step #2 – Bring your will into alignment with God's will.

Now think on this. If you don't feel well and suspect something is wrong, you get medically tested. The doctor will run certain tests, comparing and contrasting the results with what is considered "normal." When he finds something that is not aligned with certain medical standards, he knows what actions to take to bring your body into normalcy. Likewise, how do you know if you're doing right in the sight of God? In the same way: you compare and contrast your life with the Word of God. Because the Word of God is the standard, when you find yourself out of "normal" range, you can decide to realign yourself with the Word of God and make things right.

All Scripture is God-breathed and is useful for teaching, rebuking, correcting and training in righteousness, so that the man of God may be thoroughly equipped for every good work (2 Timothy 3:16-17).

As you study the Word of God, let it speak to you. Let it teach, rebuke, correct, and train you. The Word of God will show you where you should be and will reveal your shortcomings in God's eyes. In Hebrews 4:12, He makes it clear that the Word will break through and divide your soul and spirit, going deep to reveal the "thoughts and attitudes of your heart." Nothing escapes the eyes of God. Therefore, be honest with God in all things. Even what you would not tell your closest confidante, tell God. You can keep no secrets from Him because He knows you better than you know yourself.

> *For the Word of God is living and active. Sharper than any double-edged sword, it penetrates even to dividing soul and spirit, joints and marrow; it judges the thoughts and attitudes of the heart* (Hebrews 4:12).

It's very human to evaluate yourself based on your thoughts and feelings, but they are all changeable and flawed. Reality has to be weighed according to God's Word, which is unchangeable and perfect. The Word will reveal the truth about you. Forget trying to justify yourself. It won't work and it isn't necessary. In fact, all it does is slow you down and may even prevent you from reaching your divine potential altogether.

> *The heart is deceitful above all things and beyond cure. Who can understand it?* (Jeremiah 17:9)

> *For from within, out of men's hearts, come evil thoughts, sexual immorality, theft, murder, adultery, greed, malice, deceit, lewdness, envy, slander, arrogance and folly* (Mark 7:21-22).

It is clearly written that you cannot trust your feelings when it comes down to pleasing God. It deeply saddens me when people disregard the truth and make decisions based on what they personally think and feel. It's as if they are saying, "I've made up my mind, so don't confuse me with the truth." Take the time to **find** out the Word of God—it is the only true absolute in this world.

To align yourself with the Word of God, you have to ...

Step #1—See Things as They Are

Don't be afraid to acknowledge your faults before God. He knew them before you did. You can't hide them from Him. He is waiting for you to admit you are wrong. Just as the father did in the story of the prodigal son, your heavenly Father is waiting for you to return to Him. You're not perfect. (No one is.) Face the truth, the whole truth, and nothing but the truth. There is nothing wrong with being wrong—unless you're not doing anything about it. Compare yourself with the Word of God. If you are not aligned with it, make a change. Examine yourself by asking, "Does my life line up *with His Word*?" Be honest.

Now ask yourself:

- Am I really prospering?
- Am I really sickly?
- Am I really troubled?
- Am I really sinning?
- Am I really confused?
- Am I really easily angered and upset?
- Am I really in constant fear when I haven't been given a spirit of fear?
- Am I really jealous or envious?

Mark this page and from time to time come back and ask yourself these questions. They are vitally important for you to see things as they are in relation to your life.

Have you ever wondered why so many Christians can't seem to get ahead in life and are slipping behind or falling into trouble? The explanation is that they aren't standing on the Word or doing what God has commanded.

God has programmed the outcome for everything in your life already. All you have to do is go in the direction He tells you.

For those who don't stand on God's Word, the devil is only too glad to help them fall. God's Word teaches that demons don't sleep until they get you to sin. "*For they cannot sleep till they do evil; they are robbed of slumber till they make someone fall*" (Proverbs 4:16).

Don't let satan slip a virus into the program that God has for your life. The Bible is your anti-virus program. Run it daily to rid your system of the demonic attacks you face constantly.

Be on the alert for ways in which the devil is causing you to fall and is robbing you of your increase. Especially be on the lookout for the subtle ways he influences you, such as:

- Pride
- Failure to tithe
- Being lazy and wasteful instead of hard-working
- Making excuses for not doing right
- Procrastinating, hesitating, being indecisive
- Having a bad attitude
- Being unfaithful to His Church
- Being stubborn and unwilling to change
- Anything substituted in place of God's Word

As Adam and Eve walked and talked with God, they were unashamed of their nakedness. Their relationships with God and each other were completely honest and open, but when they sinned, they became aware of their nakedness and covered themselves with fig leaves. When God came looking for them, they were afraid and hid from Him.

Hiding (not admitting), like Adam and Eve did, is a good clue that you're out of fellowship with God and that you're involved in sin. Fearful of the consequences of your sin, you might even think you can hide from God. Another clue is that you justify or attempt to cover up what you have done with some attempt at a logical explanation. This just puts distance between God and you. If you are not right with God, you will not be right with the people you care about and those who care about you. **Stop hiding! Stop covering up! You cannot hide anything from God!** He knew you were going to sin before you did.

It might appear that you've gotten away with sin and deception, but sooner or later everything will *"be brought out into the open."* Your secret *will* be revealed. It is to your advantage to reveal it to

God and ask for His forgiveness and assistance to stop it, before it perhaps causes you irreparable damage.

- Do you do things that you know that aren't pleasing to God?
- Do you lie?
- Do you commit sexual sins?
- Do you lust for a married person or are you a married person who lusts for someone other than your spouse?
- Do you lust for things?
- Do you drink/smoke/do drugs?
- Do you steal?
- Do you go to fortune-tellers or study the horoscope?

For whatever is hidden is meant to be disclosed, and whatever is concealed is meant to be brought out into the open (Mark 4:22).

There is nothing concealed that will not be disclosed, or hidden that will not be made known. What you have said in the dark will be heard in the daylight, and what you have whispered in the ear in the inner rooms will be proclaimed from the roofs (Luke 12:2-3).

For God will bring every deed into judgment, including every hidden thing, whether it is good or evil (Ecclesiastes 12:14).

But if ye will not do so, behold, ye have sinned against the LORD: and be sure your sin will find you out (Numbers 32:23, KJV).

Who is to blame for your sin? When Adam and Eve were found out, they gave excuses and even blamed each other for their own decisions. Adam explained, *"The woman you put here with me—she gave me some fruit from the tree, and I ate it."* Eve reported, *"The serpent deceived me, and I ate"* (Genesis 3:12-13).

Perhaps if they had come clean, their judgment would not have been so harsh. The lesson is that it's better to admit your shortcomings. After all, these were decisions that they and YOU have made, not decisions made in the Word of God. When you take personal responsibility, God can address them and begin the corrective process in you. When you align your will to God's will, you allow Him to chart the course to your divine potential. He has given you a way out: simply confess the sin and then believe the whole truth.

> *He who conceals his sins does not prosper, but whoever confesses and renounces them finds mercy* (Proverbs 28:13).

> *If we confess our sins, he is faithful and just and will forgive us our sins and purify us from all unrighteousness* (1 John 1:9).

Let me give you another point for consideration. Adam and Eve did not accept responsibility for their sins. They passed the blame and made excuses. As a result of not being willing to admit their faults, God expelled them from paradise. On the other hand, when God confronted Cain regarding the murder of his brother and passed judgment on him, Cain appealed to God for mercy and God lightened his sentence. It is better to admit your fault than to conceal it.

> *Cain said to the Lord, "My punishment is more than I can bear. Today you are driving me from the land, and I will be hidden from your presence; I will be a restless wanderer on the earth, and whoever finds me will kill me." But the Lord said to him, "Not so; if anyone kills Cain, he will suffer vengeance seven times over." Then the Lord put a mark on Cain so that no one who found him would kill him. So Cain went out from the Lord's presence and lived in the land of Nod, east of Eden* (Genesis 4:13-16).

> *He who conceals his sins does not prosper, but whoever confesses and renounces them finds mercy* (Proverbs 28:13).

Don't be afraid to acknowledge your faults before God. It's in your own best interests to confess your sins and repent to the Lord before He has to deal with them. God encourages you to judge yourself, get right, and experience His mercy *before* He takes action. If you judge yourself first, God won't have to, and He will bless you for your confession.

It's wise to:

- **Stop making excuses.** Never again say, "The only reason I did it is because of this or that."
- **Stop lying.**
- **Admit when you do wrong.** Admit your shortcomings. Admit your failures.

There are blessings from God awaiting your submission to His will.

Let's look in 2 Samuel, chapters 11 and 12. David tried to hide his sin, but eventually it exposed him. While his men were off to war, he stayed behind in Jerusalem. While walking on his porch one day, he noticed a beautiful, married woman named Bathsheba. He sent for her and slept with her. He knew full well she was married. As a result of their affair, she became pregnant.

David had definitely gotten himself in a bind! So did he fall on his face before God and admit that he was wrong? No. He continued in it. David did the unthinkable. He had Bathsheba's husband, Uriah, murdered in order to cover his sin. Then, after Uriah's death, David took Bathsheba as his wife and she bore him a son. He should have known that a Holy God would not allow sin to go unpunished.

Yet, everything seemed to be pointing in David's favor. He had successfully concealed his sin. Of course he knew God was aware, but maybe David thought God understood his shortcomings and was being gracious. After all, God is a merciful and forgiving God.

But God wasn't going to let these secret abominations go unnoticed. The Bible tells us, *"But the thing David had done displeased the LORD"* (2 Samuel 11:27). God sent Nathan, a prophet, to David. Through Nathan, God explained all the riches and honor

He had given to David and lovingly stated that He would have given David "even more."

God's devotion to David was completely heartfelt. Unfortunately, David's devotion to God was not. David's potential was so much greater than what he had become. By concealing his sin, he hindered himself from achieving his full divine potential. The prophet said these words to him:

> *Why did you despise the word of the LORD by doing what is evil in his eyes? You struck down Uriah the Hittite with the sword and took his wife to be your own. You killed him with the sword of the Ammonites. Now, therefore, **the sword will never depart from your house**, because you despised me and took the wife of Uriah the Hittite to be your own.'* "*This is what the LORD says: '**Out of your own household I am going to bring calamity upon you. Before your very eyes I will take your wives and give them to one who is close to you, and he will lie with your wives in broad daylight**. You did it in secret, but I will do this thing in broad daylight before all Israel*'*"* (2 Samuel 12:9-12, emphasis mine).

What horrific events would follow David's trail of sins that would affect the course of his entire life and the lives of those in his household! It's obvious that concealing sin was hardly worth all the pain and suffering he reaped. He had sowed sin and reaped the whirlwind. All the things that followed were so unnecessary.

- David's daughter Tamar was raped by one of his sons, Amnon. (See 2 Samuel 13:14-16.)
- David's son Amnon was murdered by the hand of another son, Absalom. (See 2 Samuel 13:28.)
- Absalom, his beloved son, plots to steal the kingdom away from his father. (2 Samuel 15)
  - Absalom was prideful and planned to do as he pleased without respect for his father, just as David had done to God.

- David flees for his life from Absalom. (See 2 Samuel 15:14.)
  - Uriah's life was put in jeopardy, so now is David's.
- Absalom, his son, sleeps with father's concubines. (See 2 Samuel 16:22.)
  - David slept with Bathsheba in private. Now, for all to see, David's son sleeps with David's wives.
- Absalom is killed against David's wishes. (See 2 Samuel 18:15.)
  - David's general, Joab, who David told to kill Uriah, killed his son Absalom.
- The kingdom was divided and Israel deserted David. (See 2 Samuel 20:2.)
  - The kingdom rebelled, as David had rebelled against the Lord and deserted his ways.

All his life David had trouble because he tried to cover up his sin. He didn't try to line up with God's Word. If only he had been obedient, he could have had anything within God's vast and generous boundaries. If only he had known the outcome of his sins or the promise of forgiveness, he might have admitted wrongdoing right in the beginning. If only David had admitted his sins up front, maybe the penalties wouldn't have been so severe. If only David had not been so stubborn to try to cover up, if only, if only. . . .

However, David's folly can be our point of wisdom. By following David's course, you understand *"whatever is concealed is meant to be brought out into the open"* and, *"[he] who conceals his sins does not prosper."* You reap what you sow. In the end, the only way to prevent the extreme, tragic consequences of sin is to admit that you have sinned, then repent and turn away from your evildoing. Admit your sin before it reveals itself.

> *Then David said to Nathan, "I have sinned against the LORD." Nathan replied, "The LORD has taken away your sin. You are not going to die. But because by doing this you have made the enemies of the LORD show utter contempt, the son born to you will die." After Nathan had gone home,*

the LORD struck the child that Uriah's wife had borne to David, and he became ill (2 Samuel 12:13-15).

You see, sin will be punished if you don't repent within the grace of God. "I will punish their sin with the rod, their iniquity with flogging; but I will not take my love from him, nor will I ever betray my faithfulness" (Psalm 89:32-33).

God has provided you with a way out. Take it before it is too late. Why test God? Don't allow unconfessed sin to hinder you from achieving your divine potential. When you confess and repent, you receive forgiveness from your loving Father in Heaven. As you draw near and seek Him, He's right there with mercy, and His hand is ready to help you walk through your life.

Sometimes sin, even though you've repented and been forgiven, still reaps a rotten harvest. There are consequences that you can't avoid. But nevertheless, remain faithful to God and He will help you through the rotten harvest, turning it around for your good. No one except God knows how long your restoration will take. Your God is merciful. **Align yourself** with His Word. You don't want to spend your life laboring to plant and then seeing what you've planted destroyed by your sin. What a waste; then you have to plant again. You want a fruitful life! And God wants that for you, as well! Listen to Him and do as He says. Why must you experience lack and suffering to find out God knows what is right for you?

- Stop being prideful! Humble yourself.
- Stop exalting your sinful ways! Plead for His mercy
- Stop justifying! Change your ways.
- Stop hiding and ignoring your sin! Confess your sin before the Lord.
- Stop the tragic cycle! Sow good seeds for a blessed, fruitful life.

Learn from David. He wrote Psalms describing his feelings. I have included some of them for you to read and learn about David's heart during this tragic period in his life:

Blessed is he whose transgressions are forgiven, whose sins are covered. Blessed is the man whose sin the Lord does not count against him and in whose spirit is no deceit. When I kept silent, my bones wasted away through my groaning all day long. For day and night your hand was heavy upon me; my strength was sapped as in the heat of summer. Selah. Then I acknowledged my sin to you and did not cover up my iniquity. I said, "I will confess my transgressions to the Lord" —and you forgave the guilt of my sin. Selah Therefore let everyone who is godly pray to you while you may be found; surely when the mighty waters rise, they will not reach him. You are my hiding place; you will protect me from trouble and surround me with songs of deliverance. Selah. I will instruct you and teach you in the way you should go; I will counsel you and watch over you. Do not be like the horse or the mule, which have no understanding but must be controlled by bit and bridle or they will not come to you. Many are the woes of the wicked, but the Lord's unfailing love surrounds the man who trusts in him. Rejoice in the Lord and be glad, you righteous; sing, all you who are upright in heart! (Psalm 32)

Have mercy on me, O God, according to your unfailing love; according to your great compassion blot out my transgressions. Wash away all my iniquity and cleanse me from my sin. For I know my transgressions, and my sin is always before me. Against you, you only, have I sinned and done what is evil in your sight, so that you are proved right when you speak and justified when you judge. Surely I was sinful at birth, sinful from the time my mother conceived me. Surely you desire truth in the inner parts; you teach me wisdom in the inmost place. Cleanse me with hyssop, and I will be clean; wash me, and I will be whiter than snow. Let me hear joy and gladness; let the bones you have crushed rejoice. Hide your face from my sins and blot out all my iniquity. Create in me a pure heart, O God, and renew a steadfast spirit within me. Do not cast me from your presence or take your Holy Spirit from me. Restore to me the joy of

141

your salvation and grant me a willing spirit, to sustain me. Then I will teach transgressors your ways, and sinners will turn back to you. Save me from bloodguilt, O God, the God who saves me, and my tongue will sing of your righteousness. O Lord, open my lips, and my mouth will declare your praise. You do not delight in sacrifice, or I would bring it; you do not take pleasure in burnt offerings. The sacrifices of God are a broken spirit; a broken and contrite heart, O God, you will not despise. In your good pleasure make Zion prosper; build up the walls of Jerusalem. Then there will be righteous sacrifices, whole burnt offerings to delight you; then bulls will be offered on your altar (Psalm 51).

Ask yourself the following questions:

- How did David sincerely feel while he was in sin?
- How did David turn his life around?
- What wisdom can you learn from David's experience?

Confess your sins and repent quickly.

Every time you sin, run swiftly to the mercy seat. Come clean with God before things spin out of control and sin leaves a mark. The sooner, the better. Remember this:

- God forgives!
- God is pleased to give you mercy!
- God blots out your sin forever!
- God makes you holy and pure!
- God loves!
- God heals!
- God is waiting for you!

When you seek His forgiveness, God is gracious and merciful! Don't be afraid. God's nature is to forgive. A short, simple confession will do.

DIVINE POTENTIAL POWER POINTS

If you conceal your sin, you won't prosper. You won't achieve your divine potential.

1. Don't let the enemy steal from you or trap you in the dark, afraid to face the whole truth, anymore.

2. Repent of your sins before God so you can live life in freedom again. God is looking at your heart. Tell Him how you've sinned and how you feel, then ask for His mercy. What are you waiting for? Take the step now! *Pray this prayer:*

Dear God,
I've got a problem. I know I come up short in _____
areas of my life and I have sinned against you. I feel _____
_____. I'll _____ to make things right. Have
mercy on me, forgive and heal me, restore and renew me, that I may,
by Your strength, take the action to correct my ways! In Jesus' name
I pray. Amen.

Step #2—Bring Your Will Into Alignment With God's Will

Remember that from the beginning, God created man with a free will. He wanted man to be able to make his own choices. Your will overrides the will of God every time, so to achieve your divine potential, control your will. The human will is a powerful force. This is why it's called "will *power!*"

In fact, the human will can be so strong that God himself will submit to it! God allows your will for your life to be stronger than His. Why? Because He created you with the ability to choose. If He forced His will on you, you wouldn't have choice.

Now, let us understand some things about ourselves. In the original text of Genesis 1:26, the Hebrew word for "God" is *Elohim,* which is a plural form. Our Lord, our God, is *one*. Yet He is also plural; He is made up of three parts—the Trinity:

1. God the Father
2. God the Son
3. God the Holy Spirit

When God created man in His image and likeness, He also created man as a three-part being:

1. Body—the physical
2. Soul—your individuality, including your will
3. Spirit—the life in you

Your **soul** is also made up of three parts—mind, emotions, and will. We will now look at each of these components separately:

Mind

This is where you think, analyze, and make choices. People are typically controlled by their minds. Whatever the mind focuses on, the will (the other part of the soul) automatically attempts to bring to pass. Your will reacts to your thoughts. That's why it's necessary to be careful about your thinking. Don't allow the world to influence what you think. Remember, the wisdom of the world is foolishness to God.

In Philippians 4:8, the Bible tells you what things to think on so that your will aligns with God's will for your life:

- whatever is true
- whatever is noble
- whatever is right
- whatever is pure
- whatever is lovely
- whatever is admirable
- anything excellent
- anything praiseworthy

It's necessary for you to subdue and take dominion over thoughts that are contrary to the will of God. If not, the devil will be happy to give you thoughts to manipulate your mind to affect your will.

Here are three actions for you to use to take control of your mind, according to God's Word:

We demolish arguments and every pretension that sets itself up against the knowledge of God, and we take captive every thought to make it obedient to Christ (2 Corinthians 10:5).

1. Demolish every argument or reasoning that rises up against the Word of God, even if it seems logical, reasonable, and prudent.

2. Demolish every pretense or idea, feeling, desire, or passion that lifts itself up against the Word of God, even if it seems right and feels good.

3. Take captive every thought to make it obedient to Christ. It doesn't matter what you see, hear, think, or feel. It doesn't matter what anyone may say or do. Your concern is to only think and do as Christ says!

Emotions

Emotions are your feelings and passions. They can even be your ability to make distinctions; through them, you can "feel" whether something is right or wrong.

Your mind analyzes what you feel and decides what you should do. When you control your mind to meditate on God's thoughts, you influence your emotions according to the will of God.

My dear brothers, take note of this: Everyone should be quick to listen, slow to speak and slow to become angry (James 1:19).

This Scripture teaches you to:

- **Be quick to hear.** Listen with understanding to all that is said, discerning good and evil.

145

- **Be slow to speak.** Don't speak everything you're feeling or everything that's on your mind. Compare it first to the Word of God.
- **Be slow to anger.** Meditate on Scripture, take time out, and pray before you react emotionally.

Use your mind and its thoughts to take dominion over your emotions. Don't allow them to take dominion over you.

Will

The will is where the choices of your mind and the influence of your emotions are carried out—the internal force that propels you to a determined goal, where your life course is charted. Your will is acted upon by either your mind or your emotions. Once your will is set, it is hard to deter. For example, if a person is determined to sin, no one can turn him from it. If you have a set will to do righteousness, no one can turn you from it. Interestingly, the human will has no consciousness of right or wrong. It merely responds without the benefit of an internal moral barometer.

Right now you're probably controlled by either your emotions or your mind. The will is in the middle of these two. Therefore, if your thoughts or emotions are strong, they influence your will to act accordingly.

The will is the force behind any direction or change of direction you take. You can't do anything unless you first will yourself to do it. The will is the potent force that acts to bring to pass the decisions that are made by the mind. Now understand this principle: the will functions apart from the conscience if given a clear command by the mind.

A good way to understand what I am saying is to think of driving. You decide where you're going, and your will automatically leads you there. Without effort or thought, your will determines when you step on the accelerator. Let me explain it to you another way.

You say to yourself:

- "I think or feel I should exercise." Nothing happens.
- "I think or feel I will exercise." Things begin to move.
- "I exercise." The action is carried out.

I would like for you to understand the intricate distinctions among the parts of your inner self so that you're more aware of where you are in regard to the Word of God.

Have you ever played fetch with a dog that loves to retrieve a stick? Panting and wagging her tail, she waits with excited anticipation for you to throw that stick. Your will is like that dog, ready with anticipation to carry out your mind's command—whatever choice you *think* or feel *best*.

Your emotions are over here, feeling what they want, and your mind is over there, analyzing what it wants. The will continues to wait eagerly for your command. Your mind decides to either yield to your emotions or keep deliberating. Whatever your mind decides, your will—given a command—attempts to bring to pass.

Now, you can get stuck in a rut because of improper thinking that causes your will to implement actions that are contrary to your best interests. Remember, your will doesn't know right from wrong. It acts on what you're thinking at the time. Let's try to explain it another way.

Here is what a dialogue within your soul could resemble: Your alarm clock goes off—beep…beep…beep…..You don't want to get out of bed this morning. Your **emotions** say, "I'm tired. I don't want to get out of bed. Turn that alarm clock off." If your mind does not challenge your emotions, they win. Your **will** gives you the energy to push "snooze."

Then your alarm clock goes off for a second time—beep…beep… beep….Your **emotions** say, "I'm too tired. Push 'snooze' again." This time your **mind** says, "You've got to go to work." Your **emotions** say, "But this bed feels so good. Let's stay right here." Your **mind** analyzes the response from your emotions and says, "You want to eat? You want to keep your job? You've got to go to work. Get up!" Your emotions are being subdued. Your **will** then says, "Up and at 'em! We're going to work now," and gives you the energy to get up.

Then you're up and off to work. Action has taken place because you willed yourself with your mind. Your will is a powerful force when it's unleashed by your mind.

Remember, God gave you this ability to choose. He gave you a free will to decide for yourself. It is a divine gift with awesome power. If you make your mind up and choose to do good or evil, your will propels you in the direction that your mind decides. You must set a course that will affect your will, keeping in mind that once it is set in motion, it performs automatically without intervention or influence from the conscious mind. What will you choose?

The War of the Wills

Although God has given you the power to choose to do what you will, there's a tug-of-war for control. There are only four forces that affect your will:

1. The will of God. God wants you to choose His will, so He can love, communicate with, and bless you. Submission to His will is progressive and leads to the abundant life.

2. The will of the devil. He wants you to disobey God so he can steal, kill, and destroy your blessings and ultimately, you. Submission to his will leads you to a slow, painful death.

3. The will of self. You want things your way for selfish reasons. This is pride and another way that leads to death.

4. The will of others. Others want you to do things their way. This also leads to death.

You ultimately submit to the will of one of the above forces.

God is almighty, and all power is in His hands! However, in Genesis 1:27-28, it pleased God to make man in His own image. God gave man authority in the earth to subdue and rule over it, to make his own choices, and to choose whose will he will follow. Remember, your free will allows you to make a choice, and choice is a God-given right that produces either life or death. To attain your divine potential, therefore, have the will to make the choices that lead to life. If your will is so set, you automatically seek to do those things that please God.

Let's Take Another Look at Adam, Eve, the devil, and God's Will.

God placed before Adam and Eve all kinds of pleasant trees from which to eat. He excluded only one: the Tree of the Knowledge of Good and Evil. If they ate from this forbidden tree, there was a penalty—death. (See Genesis 2:15-17.) God gave man the choice to eat from any tree, including the Tree of Life.

[1] It was God's will that Adam and Eve should not eat from the Tree of the Knowledge of Good and Evil. Their decision to not do it would be their way of showing their submission to the will of God. This would position them to have the full force of God's power and presence working in them. By obeying God, they would have the ability to achieve their full divine potential.

[2] The devil's will was in direct opposition to God's. It emerges in Genesis 3:1-6. Using his will, the devil persuades Adam and Eve to eat from this forbidden tree. His main objective was to cause them to make a choice contrary to the will of God. When made, that choice would set into motion the spoken Word of God. They would die.

Eve allowed the devil to shift her mind's focus from God's will to the forbidden fruit. Watch how this affects both Adam's will and Eve's:

The devil starts to reason with Eve. Notice that the devil questions the very words spoken by God: *"Did God really say, 'You must not eat fruit from any tree in the garden'?"* The devil plants doubt in her mind. He is encouraging her to not trust the Word of God.

Then the devil blatantly opposes the very words spoken by God, *"You will not surely die,"* the serpent said to the woman. *"For God knows that when you eat of it your eyes will be opened, and you will be like God, knowing good and evil."* He provides wrong information for her to consider. He causes her to forget her identity as a human being and leads her to have a will to be like God.

Eve chooses to listen to the devil and allows her mind to consider what he said.

Eve then looks at the fruit of the tree, and her emotions begin to take priority over her mind's knowledge of what God said. She sees that it is "good for food and pleasing to the eye." She begins to visualize. Then Eve thinks on being wise and like God. This is another appeal to her emotions. And now, deceived by erroneous information, her mind yields and her will is ignited.

[3] Eve wills herself to take and eat the fruit. Her will rules over God's will for her life. Eve then uses her will to influence Adam's will and gives him the fruit.

[4] Adam yields to the will of another. He takes and eats the fruit Eve gave him. Thus Adam's will to submit to the will of another overrules God's will for his life. We can discern that Adam responds to his emotions when Eve offers him the fruit. We see no evidence of analysis. His mind is inactive; he merely responds to Eve's will.

As long as Adam and Eve were on the earth, they had the power to subdue and rule, and to choose any of the four forces for their wills. This explains how Adam and Eve had the power to resist God's will from operating in their lives. They used the divine gift of choice. Rather than subdue the serpent and take dominion over him, they submitted their wills to his.

How does this apply to you? You clearly have the ability to stop God from ruling over you by simply resisting His will and choosing your will or that of another. This is your prerogative for the time being, but a time is coming when every knee will bow and every tongue will confess that Jesus is Lord. The question is, will you do it willingly now, or will you do it when God, as the Almighty Judge of the universe, forces you and sentences you to punishment?

Adam and Eve should have chosen to submit their wills to God's will in the Word He had spoken to them. If they had chosen His will, *no* one, *no* thought, *no* reason, *no* feeling, *nothing* could have moved them to think anything different from what God had said.

They should have used the three actions cited above to control their minds and do according to God's will. This is the advice that was given by the Apostle Paul in 2 Corinthians 10:5. First, they should have chosen to destroy any reasoning or consideration that challenged what God said.

Second, they should have chosen to destroy any feelings, such as those that arose when they saw that it was good for food and pleasing to the eye. Eve never should have considered that what the devil said might be true. Adam should never have put Eve's will before God's will.

Third, Adam and Eve should have taken every thought captive, not allowing their thoughts to have free reign in their minds, subduing them, taking dominion over them, and demanding that all thoughts be in obedience to God's Word. They should have said out loud, "God said, 'You must not eat from the Tree of the Knowledge of

Good and Evil, for when you eat of it you will surely die.' Therefore, we will not eat!"

Keep it simple! Ask yourself, "Is this thought in line with the Word of God?" If not, subdue it and take dominion over it before it destroys you!

There's always a battle going on for your will. Paul makes a clear statement regarding this struggle over the will:

> *I do not understand what I do. For what I want to do I do not do, but what I hate I do. And if I do what I do not want to do, I agree that the law is good. As it is, it is no longer I myself who do it, but it is sin living in me. I know that nothing good lives in me, that is, in my sinful nature.* [Or my flesh.] *For I have the desire to do what is good, but I cannot carry it out. For what I do is not the good I want to do; no, the evil I do not want to do—this I keep on doing. Now if I do what I do not want to do, it is no longer I who do it, but it is sin living in me that does it. So I find this law at work: When I want to do good, evil is right there with me. For in my inner being I delight in God's law; but I see another law at work in the members of my body, waging war against the law of my mind and making me a prisoner of the law of sin at work within my members* (Romans 7:15-23).

Paul's mind doesn't understand. His will is doing things he doesn't intend to do. Thoughts are automatically working in Paul's mind to release his will to go forth and do.

The War Within

There are times when you want to do the right thing. But—oh, no!—you do the wrong thing *again*. You know the right thing to do and still you sin. Why? You haven't told your will to stop it! You may have thoughts that aren't according to the Word of God, but if you don't take dominion over these thoughts, you'll go out and do the wrong things. Why? Because you have not taken dominion over your will. It will do what your mind or your emotions release it to do.

After you end up doing the same thing again, you wonder, "Why did I go and do this?" Remember, your will is like playing fetch with a dog. Your will doesn't care what you tell it to go after. A stick, a ball, or piece of garbage are all the same to your will; your will simply goes after it. There are some things on which you need to put your foot down. You can't just say, "Oh, I need to stop that." You won't stop it because your will keeps on going and going and going, doing what you have given it liberty to do. You have to make clear demands on your will.

If you're doing things you don't want to do, then your will is still in gear. If you're trying to keep from sinning, but you haven't stopped, your will hasn't realized that it shouldn't be doing it. Why? Your **mind** hasn't clearly communicated it to your **will**.

The war within could sound something like this. (This could happen with any sin, but I have chosen sexual sin with a married person for this example.)

- Your **emotions** see someone they want.
- Your **will** pants, "Can I get it, can I get it?"
- Your **mind** analyzes, "Well, you know he/she is married."
- Your **emotions** admire, "But he/she looks so good."
- Your **will** pants, "Can I get it, can I get it?"
- Your **mind** relays, "But he/she has a spouse."
- Your **emotions** argue, "The spouse doesn't have to know."
- Your **will** pants, "Can I get it, can I get it?"
- Your **mind** thinks, "I don't know—we better be careful."
- Your **emotions** wander, "Think about what it'll be like."
- Your **will** pants, "Can I get it, can I get it?"
- It doesn't help that you see this person frequently.
- Your **emotions** are looking.
- Your **mind** is contemplating.
- Your **will** is ready.
- Your **will** causes you to go up to her/him and say, "You look nice today."
- Your **emotions** croon, "Ooooh!"
- Your **mind** reiterates, "He/she is married."

- Your **will** pants, "Can I get it, can I get it?"
- Your **mind** says, "Well, I don't know."
- Your **emotions** say, "Think about it."
- Your **will** pants, "Let me go! Let me go!"

This process will continue as long as your **mind** refuses to take dominion over your emotions and your will. Sooner or later, either your mind or emotions dominate, and your will reacts without any thought of the consequences. Remember, the will does not think; only the mind does. The will provides the force for a thing to happen.

In a very, very loose way, we see the same thing with God. He is the planner, the mind, if you would. Jesus is akin to the emotions. He is acquainted with what we feel. The Holy Spirit is the power of God and akin to the will. Both Jesus and the Holy Spirit are submissive to the Father and do the will of the Father.

There's a daily battle going on for your will. If the devil can't influence your mind, he'll try your emotions. Your emotions communicate with your mind. The devil will go back and forth between your mind and emotions until he can get your will released to do his will.

In this world you'll be tempted to submit your will to influences other than God. You must be aware of these invaders that try to enter in and wrestle control of your life. If these influences encourage you to do things that don't agree with the Word of God, you must immediately take authority over their influence or they'll ruin your life.

Some sources these invaders come through are:
- TV
- Music
- Friends
- Newspapers
- Loved ones (even well-meaning ones who suggest things that are contrary to the will of God)
- Advertisers who stimulate your desire to want things you don't need
- Anything that stimulates emotions that oppose God's will for your life

Align Your Will with God's!

You must choose to put your will where God's will is. As I've explained, your will is a powerful force that can't be defied by anyone except you. Even God will not override it. Therefore, *watch your step!* No matter how good your intentions are, this can be a tricky business. On one occasion, you can be submitted to God's will, and on the next occasion your will might overshadow His! God spells this out very clearly:

> *He saved them from the hand of the foe; from the hand of the enemy he redeemed them. The waters covered their adversaries; not one of them survived. Then they believed his promises and sang his praise. But they soon forgot what he had done and did not wait for his counsel. In the desert they gave in to **their craving;** in the wasteland they put God to the test. So he gave them what they asked for, but sent a wasting disease upon them* (Psalm 106:10-15, emphasis mine).

We see here that when they were committed to God, He delivered them from their enemies. But, when in their desire, they chose other things over God, He lifted His hand of protection. They forgot who God was and *"did not wait for his counsel."* They stopped seeking His will for their lives and submitting to Him. They became subject to the ways of the world and suffered for it.

We have to keep our will in line with the will of God in order to be successful. To do this we must know God's Word.

> *Do not let this Book of the Law depart from your mouth; meditate on it day and night, so that you may be careful to do everything written in it. Then you will be prosperous and successful* (Joshua 1:8).

Joshua was told to meditate on the Word so that his thinking would influence his will to act in accordance with God's will. For God's divine potential to operate in your life, you have to know His will and set your will to be in alignment with His. *"Therefore do not be foolish, but understand what the Lord's will is"* (Ephesians 5:17).

You can choose God's will and be blessed or you can choose your own will and reap the consequence of your choice—death!

To know if your will is the same as God's, study God's Word to renew your mind. Then you will be able to " … *test and approve what God's will is*" (Romans 12:2). Remember, your commitment to God's will is as strong as your commitment to study and learn His Word.

- When you don't study His Word to stay on course, your will leads you off course and away from your divine potential.
- When you forget what God says, others and other things in the world can influence your will.
- When you don't understand the Word of God, the devil is all too happy to steal the truth from you and give you lies that bring death and destruction.
- When you continue in the study of God's Word, you know His will. When you follow His will, God blesses you and improves your life progressively toward His perfect will.

How to Strengthen Your Mind to Align With God's Will

Let us consider a simple but true story and learn how to align our will with God's. In Daniel 1-3, we read about Shadrach, Meshach, and Abednego, "administrators over the province of Babylon" in approximately 850 BC. In this time, the King Nebuchadnezzar built an image of pure gold that stood ninety feet high and nine feet wide. He declared that all people throughout the kingdom were to bow down and worship the image at the sound of the "horn, flute, zither, lyre, harp, pipes, and all kinds of music." Those who did not obey the king's law would be thrown into a "fiery furnace."

The king was informed that Shadrach, Meshach, and Abednego violated his command by not bowing, so he sent for them. In the presence of the enraged king who was on the verge of throwing them into the fire, Shadrach, Meshach, and Abednego claimed that they did not need to defend themselves. Why? They were devout Jews. It was common knowledge that they wouldn't cheat, curse, lie, or worship any other gods. King Nebuchadnezzar knew who they were and he knew their beliefs.

Do your family, friends, and co-workers know who you are? Do you have a reputation for obeying and following Christ? If you do, don't be surprised that sometimes they will fashion tests to see if you are true to what you believe.

In the face of Nebuchadnezzar's fiery furnace, Shadrach, Meshach, and Abednego declared, " ... *the God we serve is able to save us from it, and he will rescue us from your hand, O king. But even if he does not, we want you to know, O king, that* **WE WILL NOT** *serve your gods or worship the image of gold you have set up"* (Daniel 3:17-18, emphasis mine).

Whether they lived or died, Shadrach, Meshach, and Abednego weren't going to bow. Why were they so strong willed? They were aware of the will of God, as He had stated in Exodus 20:1-5:

- There were to be no gods before Him.
- They were not to make any idols.
- They were not to bow down to worship them.

Knowing these things, they willed not to submit to the will of the king and committed their wills to the will of God.

Now, were Shadrach, Meshach, and Abednego born with such strong wills that they could resist such an incredible opposition? No! They disciplined themselves to develop their strong wills. By submitting to God in the simple matters, they developed the strength to yield to His will in the complex ones. We can learn from their example.

If you turn to Daniel 1:7-21 in your Bible, you will see that they had already resisted a temptation: they resolved (willed) to not defile themselves and eat royal provisions that would violate God's eating laws. Instead, they requested food that was pleasing to God. At the end of ten days, it was obvious that God had blessed their obedience. They looked healthier than all the other young men who had eaten the royal food. Because they were willing to submit to God, He caused other things to work for their good. Keep in mind that what God does for others, He will also do for you.

Shadrach, Meshach, and Abednego developed their strong wills by aligning themselves with God's Word early on when the temptation and opposition weren't so severe. And you should recognize this also: you can overcome any temptation or opposition that comes to do you wrong because God will not allow anything to come upon you that you cannot handle. If it challenges you, God has allowed it to come in your life, and you have the ability to subdue it. Do not become discouraged.

Shadrach, Meshach, and Abednego were faithful with little things and this caused them to be moved higher and higher in God and His blessings. You can do the same. Starting today, deny your will to do the things that are contrary to the Word of God. The blessings of God far exceed any blessing of the world that is against God, no matter how pleasing it might seem to your emotions.

As Shadrach, Meshach, and Abednego obeyed God's laws, He blessed them with wisdom and understanding that was equal to none. With every resistance to temptation, they were moved one step closer to their divine potential. Every resistance to temptation proved their qualification to be worthy of receiving more of the power of the presence of God. You too *can* resist temptation and prove yourself worthy!

After obeying God's Word to not bow down and worship the idol, Shadrach, Meshach, and Abednego were blessed by God's presence with them in the fire. Untouched by the scorching flames, they changed the course of history. After seeing Jesus standing with them in the furnace, King Nebuchadnezzar blessed God and issued a decree that his whole kingdom should honor their God. Shadrach, Meshach, and Abednego's divine potential was being achieved as God received glory because of their lives.

Just like Shadrach, Meshach, and Abednego, when you set it in your heart to be aligned to the will of God, you have the supernatural force of God to help you to bring it to pass. Philippians 2:13 reads, *"For it is God who works in you to will and to act according to His good purpose."* The Holy Spirit assists you. He's the "divine energizer" inside you. As you act, God helps you. He began this work in you and wants to see it come to pass to fulfill His purpose (even more than you do!).

Now, line up your will to God's will. Start by committing your will to just do some simple things in accordance with His Word, such as:

- Studying: "My will is to study fifteen minutes a day."
- Tithing: "My will is to give ten percent to God."
- Loving: "My will is to walk in love."
- Holiness: "My will is to live a holy life."

The greatest gifts of God come *after* you do what He says. As you are obedient in the simple things, special blessings are given to you to do greater things, setting you apart from others around you. You'll receive the gifts God wants you to have based on His plan for your life to propel you to the next level in Him. Every level of blessings is greater than the level before.

DIVINE POTENTIAL POWER POINTS

Remember, Know Where You Are.
You have to know where you are in relation to God's will for your life before you can move on to experience greater blessings.

The TWO STEPS that lead you to know where you are:

Step #1—See Things as They Are.
- Realize where you are.
  - What have you sown?
  - What have you reaped?
  - What in your life isn't lining up with what the Word says?
- If you conceal a sin, you won't prosper.
  - Are you hiding a sin no one else knows about? God knows!
- There's a way out!

- Learn to confess your sins and repent quickly.
- Change any tragic cycle. You don't have to live with the same sins year after year.
  - Take action according to the Word of God.
  - Change your ways.
  - Start sowing good seed. You'll reap a good harvest!

Step #2—Bring Your Will Into Alignment With God's.
- Your will power can be greater than the power of God in your life.
- You were created in His image as a three-part being – spirit, soul, and body.
- Your soul is made up of three parts—mind, emotions, and will.
  - Learn to control your mind and influence your emotions; change your will and the direction in which you're going.
  - Keep it simple! Ask yourself, "Is it in line with the Word of God?" If not, destroy it before it destroys you!
  - Your will determines your destiny. You can't do anything unless you first will to do it.
- **The War of the Wills**—The four forces that affect your choices.
  - **The will of God** – God wants you to choose His will so He can love, communicate with, and bless you.
  - **The will of the devil**—The devil wants you to disobey God so he can steal, kill, and destroy you.
  - **The will of self**—You want things your way for yourself.
  - **The will of others**—Others want you to do things their way.
- **His will or your will?**
  - Your commitment to God's will is as strong as your commitment to study and learn God's Word.
- How do you strengthen your will to choose God's will?
  - Memorize scripture.
  - Make a commitment to know God's will
  - Submit your will to God's will daily.

CHAPTER 7

Performance Principle Number Three

Inquire of God About Your Divine Potential

Hearing From God Through Prayer

Satan does not want us to know that we are children of God, who are invested with divine potential to do exceedingly great things in partnership with the Lord. He seeks to keep us ignorant of our potential so that we will not have faith in God's power, and will live weak and defeated lives. We now understand that we must study God's Word to find out who we truly are in the sight of God, and then align ourselves with God's Word so that we may experience more of God's presence. Additionally, satan does not want us to know about our divine potential and God's designs for our life.

Therefore, we do everything necessary to determine what God has to say about our potential in life so as not to waste time wandering aimlessly without accomplishing the will of God. In our lives we are faced with many decisions—some great, some small. Where we are today is the result of the choices we have made to date. Our future is determined by the choices we make today.

There are many questions. What should I do now? Which way should I turn? What job should I take? Which school should I choose? What relationship should I have? What relationships should I reject? How should I spend my time?

You may not know today what you should do with your life, but God does, and He desires to reveal to you what you can become.

How will God communicate your personal revelation to you? First, ask and seek God for a revelation. He desires for us to acknowledge Him and receives all the glory when we become all He intends for us to be. God can open your eyes in many different ways. Here are just a few:

- In prayer, fasting, and repentance. (See Daniel 9:21; Daniel 10:2-3.)
- While reading, studying, and meditating on the Word. (See Daniel 9:2.)
- In church through worship, fellowship, and accountability to others in ministry. (See 1 Corinthians 11-13.)
- Through other godly people:
  - Godly friends. (See Proverbs 27:9.)
  - Godly counselors. (See Proverbs 24:6.)
  - Ministers of the Lord, such as preachers, teachers, prophets, evangelists, and apostles. (See Ephesians 4:11-16.)
- Through dreams and visions. (See Joel 2:28-29.)
- In listening to God's still, small voice. (See 1 Kings 19:11-13.)
- With inner knowing by the Spirit. (See John 10:4.)

As you see, God can speak to you in many ways. Principally, though, you're to call Him to do so through an ancient discipline—prayer.

Receive Revelation From God Primarily Through Prayer

Prayer is communication and connection with your heavenly Father. Prayer is where you meet God face-to-face. God uses His Word to draw us closer to Him. Through prayer, we draw God closer to us. Prayer personalizes our relationship with our heavenly Father. Having learned His voice from the study of His Word, we sharpen our skills by listening and communicating with Him in our prayer time.

Sincere Spirit-filled prayer connects us to the mighty hand of God. Prayer helps correct your thoughts, words, and actions by replacing worry and doubt. Mighty things come into existence—things you never dreamed of or imagined. His presence energizes your life and gives you strength you never knew was available to you.

Prayer may seem simple enough, but don't underestimate the seeming simplicity of it. Prayer is power! God uses the simple things to confound the wise. When you pray the Word and communicate the truth from within you, there's an intimacy with your heavenly Father. This intimacy creates a place of trust where visions and dreams are made reality. You see God and He comforts you to know that He is always with you.

In genuine and sincere prayer, you aren't out to please the world or others. You pray for what God desires, not what you want. You pray to seek and please God. And when God is pleased, anything—I mean *anything*—is possible!

In prayer, remind God of the Word you have studied. Set your mind in agreement with the will of God for your life. Pray, *"Our Father in heaven, ... your kingdom come, your will be done on earth as it is in heaven"* (Matthew 6:9-10). Pray for God's will to occur in your life. His will for your life is greater than you ever imagined, and with your permission, He will lift you to ever-increasing heights in life. He is ready to reveal His perfect will for your life.

When praying, get to a place where you can hear from God. Get alone where there are no disturbances or distractions—in a prayer room, closet, shower, your car, a tree, on a mountaintop, or near a flowing stream. Pray also with others in prayer meetings, praise and worship sessions, or church meetings and Bible studies.

Inquire of Him in prayer specifically for a revelation of what you can become. Ask Him what He created you for. Expect an answer. He will reveal an image of what you can be when you submit to His will for your life. If you accept His revelation, you will move toward your true destiny in Christ and away from the bondage of limited human expectations.

God works in you to deliver you from incorrect thoughts, words, and actions. Don't be afraid to believe in the Word God gives you. Have faith in God's vision for you, even if it seems to transcend your ability or natural means. When you submit to God, your ability is no longer limited to your skills; you have tapped into the awesome force of His power for your life.

Think on this:

- It wasn't the disciples' ability that fed the 5,000.
- It wasn't the Israelites ability that brought down the walls at Jericho.
- It wasn't Peter's great fishing skill that caught so many fish that the boat started to sink.
- It wasn't Elijah's ability to call down fire from heaven.
- It wasn't Daniel's ability to shut the lion's mouth.

No. In all of these situations, it was the power of God working through willing vessels.

When you submit to the revelation of what God has for your life and determine within yourself to achieve it, nothing seen or unseen can stop you from getting there. Whether you are rich or poor, black or white, educated or uneducated, your beginning may be humble, but your future will be prosperous as you submit to what God has prepared for you. Recognize that your promotion is not dependent upon what man does, but it rests in the hands of Almighty God. Be confident and faithful; He will promote you in due season.

Prayer activates God's energy within you. As you pray to Him, God speaks to you. He speaks to your natural and spiritual limitations. He reduces their control in your life and orders your footsteps into the ways that will achieve your divine potential. As you learn to hear from Him spiritually, His revelations transform your life in astounding ways. Remember, His Word created the universe, and as you speak back and forth with Him, the conversation will alter your environment and redefine everything in your world.

It is also important for you to realize that when God speaks to you through prayer, it is His Word that will provide nourishment for your spirit, soul, and body. His Word, whether you receive it as you read it in the Bible or as He speaks to you in prayer, is life and health to your whole being. Just one simple revelation from God is enough to radically change your life for the better. God has honored you to be able to enter His presence through prayer. Take advantage of the opportunity.

As you pray, don't be afraid to open yourself up and be real with God. You don't have to use a spiritual tone to talk to Him. Just speak to Him as you would to an intimate friend. He knows you better than anyone else does. You have nothing to hide. God desires for you to share your worries with Him; He cares about your concerns: *"Cast all your anxiety on him because he cares for you"* (1 Peter 5:7).

When to Pray

God's Word says that David was a man after God's own heart. What can we learn from him about inquiring of God in prayer?

- *In the morning, O Lord, you hear my voice; in the morning I lay my requests before you and wait in expectation.* (Psalm 5:3)
  - Therefore, pray in the morning. Morning comes only once a day.
- *O Lord, the God who saves me, day and night I cry out before you.* (Psalm 88:1)
  - Now, pray at night. This means you should pray in the morning and in the night.
- *Evening, morning and noon I cry out in distress, and he hears my voice.* (Psalm 55:17)
  - Therefore, pray morning, noon and night. How many times per day? At least three.

What about other scriptures? *Pray continually.* (1 Thessalonians 5:17)

What About Jesus?

Very early in the morning, while it was still dark, Jesus got up, left the house and went off to a solitary place, where he prayed (Mark 1:35).

One of those days Jesus went out to a mountainside to pray, and spent the night praying to God (Luke 6:12).

In What Position Should You Pray?

We have seen examples in scripture of prayer from all types of positions and postures: standing, seated, lying down, or kneeling. It doesn't matter. God will hear you if your heart is right.

Should Your Prayers Be Formal or Informal?

Formal, ritualized prayers or informal, spontaneous prayers are equal. The most important point is to pray with a sincere heart. Your prayer must be meaningful.

How Should I Pray?

Pray believing. Forgive others for any sin they have committed against you, and assure that you are aligned with the Word of God. One more final thing: pray in the name of Jesus. Say this as you conclude: "In Jesus' name I pray. Amen."

> *In that day you will no longer ask me anything. I tell you the truth, my Father will give you whatever you ask in my name. Until now you have not asked for anything in my name. Ask and you will receive, and your joy will be complete* (John 16:23-24).

What Will You Become?

You'll become more than you ever thought or even imagined you could be! God has a plan and purpose for you and you're *perfectly* made to fulfill it. You will experience a spiritual transformation followed by a natural transformation toward His purpose.

Almighty God is the only one who knows what He created you to be. He designed you with unique talents, gifts, and skills that make you perfectly suited for this specific purpose in life. Look at the world around you. All the things created by Him fulfill their purposes almost effortlessly and flawlessly. Look at the animal kingdom; each creature is perfectly made for its purpose in life.

He will reveal your purpose to you if you ask Him. Then, when you examine your life, you will see that you, too, have been empowered all along to accomplish it.

Let's talk for a moment about this "revelation" of your purpose. It's God's Word just for you—a divine communication to tell you something you didn't know. Revelation means "vision." When you have a vision, you have a clear direction and drive to achieve all that God has planned for you. And when you have a God-given vision, God gives you all the provisions you need to accomplish it.

Where there is no vision, the people perish (Proverbs 29:18, KJV).

Dr. Martin Luther King had a dream, a vision that focused the direction for his life and propelled him toward a great destiny that changed the course of the twentieth century. The zeal for something bigger than himself motivated Dr. King to walk away from hindering areas in his life and toward a more superior life-style that would support his dream and his vision. He refused to allow the words of the people around him to affect what he felt God had called him to do in life. He pressed on with the words, "I have a dream."

It's time for you to receive the revelation of what you can become. To do this, you may have to sacrifice many worldly relationships and desires. You are called to replace the "good things" in your life with the "God things." He delights in your efforts to discover His will for your life and eagerly desires to reveal it to you.

Call to me and I will answer you and tell you great and unsearchable things you do not know (Jeremiah 33:3).

He is saying that He will reveal things that you do not yet know, including His plan for your life. For instance, in the scripture below we see how God's Spirit reveals to us things we cannot naturally know that are in the mind of God.

However, as it is written: "No eye has seen, no ear has heard, no mind has conceived what God has prepared for those who love him"—but God has revealed it to us by his Spirit. The Spirit searches all things, even the deep things of God. For who among men knows the thoughts of a man except the man's spirit within him? In the same way no one knows the thoughts of God except the Spirit of God. We have not received the spirit of the world but the Spirit who is from God, that we may understand what God has freely given us. This is what we speak, not in words taught us by human wisdom but in words taught by the Spirit, expressing spiritual truths in spiritual words. The man without the Spirit does not accept the things that come from the Spirit of God, for they are foolishness to him, and he cannot understand them, because they are spiritually discerned (1 Corinthians 2:9-14).

Plan to Obey God's Way

Your revelation from God now grows into a plan to bring it into existence. When God gives you a revelation of your divine potential, it's His plan for your life. He knows what steps you need to take to accomplish it. He's ready to lead you through the process. You must have a plan.

> *Suppose one of you wants to build a tower. Will he not first sit down and estimate the cost to see if he has enough money to complete it? For if he lays the foundation and is not able to finish it, everyone who sees it will ridicule him, saying, "This fellow began to build and was not able to finish"* (Luke 14:28-30).

Because of some of the disciplines you've already learned, you find that your ability to hear from God is even clearer now. He speaks to you every step of the way. *"Your ears will hear a voice behind you, saying, 'This is the way; walk in it'"* (Isaiah 30:21).

You might ask, "How do I get a plan that is specific to my revelation?" It's simple. The same way you got the revelation. You ask God! Remember to go daily before the Lord, inquire, and listen for His plan.

> *Now listen, you who say, "Today or tomorrow we will go to this or that city, spend a year there, carry on business and make money." Why, you do not even know what will happen*

tomorrow. What is your life? You are a mist that appears for a little while and then vanishes. Instead, you ought to say, "If it is the Lord's will, we will live and do this or that" (James 4:13-15).

- *Before* you accept a job, ask God if this is the job He has for you.
- *Before* you decide on a career, pray over it until you know God's will.
- *Before* you decide on a college and a major, seek God's plan for your life.
- *Before* you buy a car or house, ask and listen to God.
- *Before* you buy anything or make a big change or decision in your life, pray over and through it.
- *Before* you decide on a relationship of any type, ask God first.

You might have been walking around through life without ever looking for God's plan for you. I want you to come to know that God's promise to you is that when you seek Him with your whole heart, you'll find Him and His plan for you. God determines your place. No one can take it away from you. Nothing can stop you.

Here is what you need to know. The Spirit of God gives you revelation of what you can become. You must therefore learn to be sensitive to His Spirit so that you will hear His voice when He speaks to you, leading and directing you to the things that will cause you to achieve your divine potential.

God said this to the Prophet Isaiah in regards to His direction in our lives:

> *Whether you turn to the right or to the left, your ears will hear a voice behind you, saying, "This is the way; walk in it"* (Isaiah 30:21).

This is God's way of telling us that He shall speak to us and lead us in the paths that we should go by His Spirit. Jesus said this to us, *"The Spirit gives life; the flesh counts for nothing. The words I have spoken to you are spirit and they are life"* (John 6:63).

Remember, the *"Spirit searches all things, even the deep things of God"* (1 Corinthians 2:10).

Throw away bad thoughts and desires, negative and false emotions, evil and contentious words, and wasteful and destructive actions. Trash anything and everything that doesn't line up with God's Word. Be careful not to allow yourself to think on anything that is contrary to His written Word, no matter how innocent it may seem. Study God's Word and personalize every promise of good things and blessings for your life. Remember, God is no respecter of persons. What He did for the people in the Bible, He will also do for you. Expectation creates manifestation.

Remember, the flesh counts for nothing. It will pass away. So, set your mind on the things of the Spirit and know that you can do all things through Christ who strengthens you.

Set aside time daily to dedicate entirely to God. Spend this time in prayer, fasting, and studying God's Word. Find time also to spend fellowshipping with other sincere Christians.

In reading Daniel 10-12, we discover how Daniel was given an awe-inspiring revelation from God. Chapter 10 starts where Daniel received from God a revelation of a great war, but didn't know the interpretation of it. So, Daniel set his mind to gain an understanding of it by inquiring of God. He humbled himself before God. He asked and petitioned Him sincerely for twenty-one days—and received the interpretation.

This communication is also God's will for your life. He will gladly reveal things to you when you genuinely seek Him with your whole heart. Is this not what He has told us in Jeremiah 33:3? *"Call to me and I will answer you and tell you great and unsearchable things you do not know."*

We can learn a lot from Daniel about how to show God sincerity in our quest for revelation. What becomes clear from our study is that Daniel took control over his flesh.

- He disciplined himself to set aside time for God for three weeks.
- He mourned and prayed consistently throughout this time.
- He deprived himself of choice food—no meat or wine.

- He used no lotions to comfort his flesh.

Daniel was the only one who saw the interpretation unfold. When the presence of the Lord came, the others fled in fear and left Daniel alone "gazing at this great vision."

Recognize and understand that others won't always appreciate your vision. They can't. The things of God are awesome, and they provoke fear in those who lack intimacy with Him. They aren't seeking or listening to the Word of God. Most people will seek only man's ways. The ways of God will seem like foolishness to them.

You must always remember that your heavenly Father loves you, and wants to bless you with good things. As you listen to His voice, He progressively leads you into the ways of blessings.

God will calm your fears and strengthen you. Listen to how a messenger of God communicates to Daniel: *"Do not be afraid, O man highly esteemed,"* he said. *"Peace! Be strong now; be strong"* (Daniel 10:19). Daniel was strengthened by these words and replied, *"Speak, my lord, since you have given me strength"* (Daniel 10:19).

When God and Abraham communicated, Abraham expressed his fears and questions to the Lord:

> *After this, the word of the LORD came to Abram in a vision: "Do not be afraid, Abram. I am your shield, your very great reward." But Abram said, "O Sovereign LORD, what can you give me since I remain childless and the one who will inherit my estate is Eliezer of Damascus?" And Abram said, "You have given me no children; so a servant in my household will be my heir"* (Genesis 15:1-3).

Abraham was thinking in the natural and, therefore, he was limiting his own potential and negating the power of God. I always like to share with my congregation this thought: *See things as they are; now see things as they are.* Simply put, I am encouraging them to see things as they are in the natural, but then to see things as they really are in the spiritual. The real truth of the matter is that the things in the spirit are the *real* reality. The spiritual reality will ultimately cancel out the natural reality. Once you capture the vision in the spiritual realms and begin speaking it in the natural, it is compelled to manifest in the natural. God created us and knows that if we can see a thing in the spirit realm, we can bring it to pass in the natural.

Watch as the Lord answers Abraham's concerns and leads him even further into his divine purpose: to become "A Father of Many Nations."

> *Then the word of the LORD came to him: "This man will not be your heir, but a son coming from your own body will be your heir." He took him outside and said, "Look up at the heavens and count the stars—if indeed you can count them." Then he said to him, "So shall your offspring be." Abram believed the LORD, and he credited it to him as righteousness* (Genesis 15:4-6).

Notice, Abraham is concerned with being childless, having no heir. God takes the time to address his concerns and then goes a step beyond and explains to Abraham that his offspring will be so numerous that he won't be able to count them.

- God wanted Abraham to visualize an image of the infinite stars.
- God gave him a vision, which would affect Abraham's thoughts.
- God reiterated the vision to Abraham repeatedly to help him grasp his potential.
  - God called Abraham the *"father of many nations."* (See Genesis 17:4.)
  - God said that He would increase Abraham's numbers. (See Genesis 17:2.)
  - God blessed Abraham: *"I will make your name great"* (Genesis 12:2).
  - God stated, *"I will make you very fruitful; … and kings will come from you"* (Genesis 17:6).
  - God changed Abram's name to Abraham, meaning *"father of a multitude of nations."* Every time anyone called his name, Abraham was reminded of the vision.

- God showed him the land He would give to Abraham and his offspring. (See Genesis 13:14-15.)
- God reiterated that Abraham's offspring would be *"like the dust of the earth;"* no one would be able to count them. (See Genesis 13:16.)
- God rewarded Abraham's obedience, *"and through your offspring all nations on earth will be blessed, because you have obeyed me"* (Genesis 22:18).

Notice how many times God repeated the vision to Abraham. It is the repetition of God's Word in your life that transforms your environment. I wonder how many nights Abraham sat alone, staring at the stars and thinking of the vision. Abraham watched and waited a long time for this vision to come to pass—and it finally did.

God has a vision waiting especially for you, just as He had one for Abraham. Go to your Father in Heaven and ask Him for your revelation of what you can become. He will try you for a while to strengthen your faith and draw you closer to Him. Don't become disappointed when you don't get clarity in the beginning. Keep pressing on. He will certainly respond. God always answers prayer.

Picture Jacob in your mind now. Here was a man who wrestled with God, refusing to let go until He blessed him. You must be the same way. Keep holding on until you get the answer. Jesus has taught us that men must always pray and not faint. Keep going back again and again in prayer. Pray in the morning, pray in the noonday, and pray when you go to bed at night. Remember that you're asking God for His will for your life. You are seeking to live your life to His glory. He will reveal His will for you. He desires to do this because the harvest is plentiful, but the laborers are few. He wants you to serve Him. Your joy will be in serving Him.

When you receive it, and you most certainly will, **MAP!** **(Meditate, Apply and Perform** it.) Speak it out loud. Share it with your intimate friends. Never let it go. Refuse to accept anything less than what God has revealed to you.

Just as Abraham was, you have to be persistent, diligent, and committed to His revelation. And, just as Abraham was, you'll be richly rewarded by the manifestation of your divine potential.

Trusting what God says about you, you'll receive the eternal blessings of the Lord.

How Do You Receive a Revelation?

Often you'll receive revelations in parts—one piece at a time, almost like a puzzle. You don't see the big picture until your divine potential is fulfilled or almost complete. Or God could give you the big picture and then hand you revelation piece-by-piece until the puzzle's complete.

Don't limit God with regard to how you have to receive a revelation. Don't bother trying to piece together the vision by your own means. God's ways supersede ours. If you want the pieces to fit together perfectly, seek His ways and Him.

What to do When You Receive the Revelation

Ask God to be certain that your revelation is from Him and not from your own desires.

- Wait for a confirmation through two or three witnesses to establish the revelation. These witnesses may be people that God puts before you through divine appointments. They might not even realize that God is using them specifically to confirm His Word to you. He also might confirm it with circumstances or special situations.
- Once you have received your revelation of who you are to become, cover it in prayer and allow God to refine it as time passes. *"Do not be anxious about anything, but in everything, by prayer and petition, with thanksgiving, present your requests to God"* (Philippians 4:6).
- Most important, be certain your revelation lines up with Scripture. If not, you didn't receive it from God.
- Continue to study and meditate on the Word; search for related topics in the Bible to confirm your revelation.
- Stay concentrated and focused on what God has said and is saying, and where you are going. Meditate on the revelation.
- Write it down.

- Wait on the Lord to reveal more as you go along. (See Psalm 27:14.)
- Give thanks and praise for where you are. (See Psalm 138:2.)
- Have faith that the revelation will manifest in the natural.

Now be careful, and test the spirits to see if they are from God. Some things look like blessings, but are really traps in disguise. When satan realizes that you are about to receive a blessing, he will send a decoy to cause you to miss "the real McCoy." With excitement, you'll jump right in, thinking these things are from God. Yet, in reality they're from the devil. He knows you won't seek God for the truth if you want the blessing so badly.

You might be trying to hold onto something that really isn't from God—it's your own desire! God might be trying to give you something better. Accept what God speaks to you, even if He asks you to give it away, leave it alone, stay here, or go there.

Always remember, God won't contradict His written Word. Don't be deceived by your own desires or those who speak opposite to His Word. Let His written Word be your final authority!

NOW HEAR THIS! No matter what you feel, think, perceive, conceive, dream, sense, reveal, observe, see, concoct, or discern—no matter where it comes from—if you can't back it up with Scripture, forget it. It's *not* of God!

You might respond, "I'm asking God for help, but He's not answering." Maybe God has already answered you in His Word. Have you looked for it? Who are you seeking for your answers? How many people are calling the psychic hotlines? "Hello, Madam Madonna, what should I do in this situation?" Seek wise counsel. (See Psalm 1:1). How many people with marriage problems ask advice from friends who are divorced or living promiscuous lives? Watch who *you* hang around with, and avoid wrong relationships. (See 2 Corinthians 6:17-18.)

Inquire of God and take the necessary precautions to make certain that the revelation is from God. This might take a little more time. Yet, when you're certain, you can be bold and courageous, knowing that you will prosper in the thing that God has set you to do.

Once again ...

- Inquire of God.
- Wait for two or three confirmations.
- Pray about it again.
- Be certain that it aligns with the Word.
- MAP it! (Meditate, Apply and Perform)

When you're convinced that the revelation is God's, move toward it. Continually let God set and chart your course! Stay concentrated and focused on what God said and is saying, and where you're going. Now, let's look at the remaining points.

Write the Revelation Down and
Keep a Journal of Your Progress Toward It

> *And the LORD answered me, and said,* **Write the vision,** *and make it plain upon tables, that he may run that readeth it* (Habakkuk 2:2, KJV, emphasis mine).

When God gives you directions to follow or answers your questions, write them down! Writing down the Word is commanded of God:

1. *"Write them on the tablet of your heart"* (Proverbs 7:3).

2. *"Write them on doorframes of your houses and on your gates"* (Deuteronomy 6:9).

Writing in your journal honors Him. You're communicating that what He said to you is precious and worthy of your time and effort. The Almighty God honors you when you honor Him.

Here are a few guidelines that will help you focus your journal and get the most out of it:

1. Write down circumstances, events, places, symbols, and words God speaks to you.

2. Write down answers, situations, and solutions so you can recollect how God has dealt with you in the past. You may need these solutions for future circumstances. You may begin to see a

pattern in your life that needs correcting. You may see a pattern in your life that leads to victory!

3. Write down how God delivered you. God told Moses to write down the victory against Amalek where Aaron and Hur held up the hands of Moses. (See Exodus 17:14.)

4. Also, keep things as memorials or signs. See how the Bible tells us to use them:

When God stopped the flow of Jordan so the Israelites could pass over with the ark, He instructed them to take up twelve stones for " *... a sign among you. In the future, when your children ask you, 'What do these stones mean?' tell them that the flow of the Jordan was cut off before the ark of the covenant of the Lord. When it crossed the Jordan, the waters of the Jordan were cut off. These stones are to be a memorial to the people of Israel forever"* (Joshua 4:4-7).

5. As you write, the Holy Spirit will guide you to your own revelation.

6. As you write, abundant life will seep into your eyes and ears, making its way to your heart. Out of your heart are the issues of life. (See Proverbs 4:23.) When you hear with your heart, your faith grows. When your faith grows, all things are possible.

7. Write down any situation that you may be facing, i.e. complaints, problems, etc.

8. Search God's Word regarding your situation.

9. Write down what the Word says, so that you can follow it.

10. Write accurately, and don't try to fill in the blanks. Don't add or remove anything. (It's easy to confuse your own desires with God's desires for you.)

11. Review your situations and make certain you are steadfast to the Word's instructions, waiting for the Lord's next move.

Once you have your journal going, follow these **Four Rs** and they'll empower you to seize your revelation:

1. **R**ead it!
2. **R**emember it!
3. **R**eplay it over again and over again!
4. **R**un with it!

BE CAREFUL, DON'T NEGATE!

Now let me ask you? Do you have doubt about what I am saying? You aren't alone. In Mark 9:17-29, we read about a man in the crowd who brought his son who was, " ... *possessed by a spirit that has robbed him of speech. Whenever it seizes him, it throws him to the ground. He foams at the mouth, gnashes his teeth and becomes rigid ... From childhood ... It has often thrown him into fire or water to kill him"* (Mark 9:17-22).

The boy's father said to Jesus, *"I asked your disciples to drive out the spirit, but they could not"* (Mark 9:18).

This situation, which endured for most of the young boy's life, seemed out of control and looked utterly hopeless. So what did Jesus say to the father? *"Everything is possible for him who believes"* (Mark 9:23). In other words, Jesus told him, "You've come to Me and nothing is impossible with Me if you believe." Immediately the father exclaimed, *"I do believe; help me overcome my unbelief!"* (Mark 9:24).

Jesus told the man to believe for the impossible. The man's doubt was natural, but God deals in the Spirit, and the Spirit is supernatural (above the natural). He was teaching this man the same way He taught Abraham and others: overcoming natural impediments with a spiritual weapon—faith!

Even the disciples struggled with unbelief. In private the disciples asked Jesus why they were unable to deliver the young boy. *"And Jesus said unto them, Because of your unbelief: for verily I say unto you, If ye have faith as a grain of mustard seed, ye shall say unto this mountain, Remove hence to yonder place; and it shall remove; and nothing shall be impossible unto you. Howbeit this kind goeth not out but by prayer and fasting"* (Matthew 17:20-21, KJV).

When you pray and fast, as Jesus instructed the disciples to do, you starve your flesh and feed your faith. Your natural senses— seeing, hearing, tasting, smelling, and feeling—become weakened. Your faith strengthens. You become attuned to the spiritual ways of discerning and knowing God's will. There is another world that supersedes and orders our world—the spiritual world. Prayer gives you the ability to reach into the spiritual realm and bring into your natural reality the things that are revealed there. Remember, God is Spirit. We worship Him in spirit and truth.

Keeping the Negative Out

When the mind becomes quiet in prayer, wrong thoughts and feelings might intrude. Therefore, it's important to:

- Deny evil thoughts of being a failure, incapable, or a loser. Deny thoughts focused on worry, revenge, jealousy, unforgiveness, sickness, or disease.
- Deny words that support evil thoughts.
- Deny actions that follow evil thoughts and words.
- Remember to take captive every thought and bring it into obedience to Christ.

It doesn't matter how awful your situation is at this moment. Jesus is right there with you to help overcome your unbelief. Ask the Lord for His strength. He will carry you through to the place of miracles. He is waiting for you to come to Him in prayer.

Nine Ways to Overcome Doubt

1. Elevate the Word over your situation, and you'll be kept in perfect peace. (See Matthew 4:4, 7, 10; Isaiah 26:3.)

2. Confess and believe in the Word. (See Psalm 34; Numbers 14.)

3. Recognize your partnership with God. (See Matthew 10:20.)

4. Remember that you're God's workmanship. You were created in Christ Jesus to do good works, which God prepared in advance for you to do. (See Ephesians 2:8-10.) Be confident that God will carry the good work in you on to completion. (See Philippians 1:5-6.)

5. Remain calm. Don't panic! The devil thrives during your times of fear—remember you have the ultimate victory! God is still in control and He has a plan for your life. Get in it!

I was young and now I am old, yet I have never seen the righteous forsaken or their children begging bread (Psalm 37:25).

Look at life as if you were playing a game of cards. God, as the dealer, deals you all the right cards, guaranteeing that you'll win in the end. Yet, He may allow you to lose a hand or two along the way. Why? To test your confidence and build your faith in Him, and to show you that no matter how bleak things might appear, He can turn them around for your good. Can you believe Him when He tells you that you'll win in the end?

6. Be confident of deliverance. (See Isaiah 55:11; Psalm 40:1-5; Psalm 27:1-6.)

7. Recognize that God is your Father. (See Romans 8:14-15.) You have received the Spirit of Sonship. You haven't been given the spirit of fear, but of power, love, and a sound mind. (See 2 Timothy 1:7). When you receive His spirit, you have the right to enter into His Kingdom and realize all the spiritual blessings you have right now and then speak those spiritual blessings into your natural reality for the present time.

8. Since God is your Father, meditate on His name:

a. *Abba* – Your father
b. *Elohim* – God of gods, Lord of lords—Holy, Holy, Holy
c. *El-Shaddai* – Almighty God
d. *Jehovah-Jireh* – Your Provider
e. *Jehovah-Rophe* – Your Healer
f. *Jehovah-Nissi* – Your Banner for Victory
g. *Jehovah-M'Kaddesh* – Your Sanctifier
h. *Jehovah-Shalom* – Your Peace
i. *Jehovah-Tsidkenu* – Your Righteousness
j. *Jehovah-Rohi* – Your Shepherd
k. *Jehovah-Shammah* – Your ever-present help in times of need
l. The Great *I AM* – He is the great *I Am*, there is nothing He cannot handle.

9. Take authority over your situation. (See 2 Corinthians 10:4.)

- Understand that your answer may not come the way you think.
- Know that He delivers even from death and has a revelation of what you can become.

Prayer and fasting will empower you to believe God when nothing else can!

As you pray and fast, you become spiritually stronger. You are empowered to see things from God's perspective, hear God's will, and be sensitive to God's Spirit. Prayer and fasting elevate you to a place where things could look utterly hopeless, and yet you have faith to believe for the "impossible!" Faith never fails. "Impossible" is a word for unbelievers. There is nothing impossible for one who believes. Almighty God assures us of this.

In some areas of your life, prayer and fasting will be the only way out. As Jesus taught the disciples, prayer and fasting will stomp out your unbelief, making room for your faith to grow. Jesus taught that if you have faith even *"as a grain of mustard seed,"* you can speak to those areas and they will be removed! (See Matthew 17:20-21, KJV.)

When God reveals your extraordinary future to you, believe! Don't ignore it because it seems unbelievable or you think it is impossible. Change your thinking!

- Confidently think and believe that since you're earnestly seeking God, He has a reward for you. (See Hebrews 11:6.)
- Confidently think and believe that anything's possible for you with God. (See Mark 9:23.)
- Confidently think and believe that the Lord will deliver you from all of your troubles and afflictions. (See Psalm 34:19.)
- Confidently think and believe that you can handle any temptation. (See 1 Corinthians 10:13.)
- Confidently think and believe that God has provided a way out. (See 1 Corinthians 10:13.)
- Confidently think and believe that you've received whatever you have asked for in prayer. (See Mark 11:24.)
- Confidently think and believe that what you say in prayer to God will happen. You can move mountains out of your life. (See Mark 11:23.)
- Finally, confidently think and believe—simply because *God says so!*

As you pray and believe His Word, the Lord orders your thoughts, words, and actions to line up with and reveal His divine purpose for your life. And the Lord sets you on the course to complete fulfillment in reality of your divine potential. Your prayer and meditation work powerfully together to set you in position to receive His revelation of what you can become!

May the words of my mouth and the meditation of my heart be pleasing in your sight, O LORD, my Rock and my Redeemer (Psalm 19:14).

Now Hear This!

You, as a believer in Christ, have **already** been given a plan from God. God wants you to move forward in that plan and fulfill His will in the earth to:

1. Be in God's image.
2. Be blessed.
3. Be fruitful.
4. Multiply His image.
5. Replenish.
6. Subdue.
7. Take dominion.

Second, and equally important, you have a plan that is specific to your life. You were created with specific talents and gifts to fulfill this plan. Your God-given revelation or vision should be planned out according to God's will specifically for you.

If you really want God's plan, get on your knees and pray, "Lord, give me your plan for getting over there."

With God, calculate the cost before you begin implementing the plan. Then take your time to earnestly develop the plan, write it down, and discipline yourself to follow it. *"Write down the revelation and make it plain on tablets so that a herald may run with it"* (Habakkuk 2:2).

1. Write out a daily schedule of what you should accomplish.

2. Set up a well-thought-out system with checkpoints to follow along the way.

3. Check off completed points to make sure you're proceeding according to God's plan.

4. Include goals (do not write them in stone; allow God to direct you as He chooses).

- *Immediate goals*—what do you hope to accomplish each day?
- *Short-term goals*—for the next week to twelve months.
- *Intermediate goals*—for the next five years.
- *Long-term goals*—for the next ten years and beyond.

5. Create a back-up plan in case your first plan doesn't go exactly as you thought or comes up short. Be courageous enough to admit it when things don't go as expected.

Keep your focus on God and permit Him to alter your plans as He sees fit. Often our understanding of what God says needs to be adjusted. Therefore, always be open to hear His voice.

God will give additional revelation on how to accomplish His plan through His Holy Spirit as you:

- state the vision again and again, and
- continue in a close, intimate relationship with God.

But when he, the Spirit of truth, comes, he will guide you into all truth. He will not speak on his own; he will speak only what he hears, and he will tell you what is yet to come (John 16:13).

"No eye has seen, no ear has heard, no mind has conceived what God has prepared for those who love him"—but God has revealed it to us by his Spirit. The Spirit searches all things, even the deep things of God (1 Corinthians 2:9).

God will reveal what you need to know when you need to know it, not before.

Live by Faith

But the just shall live by his faith (Habakkuk 2:4, KJV).

When you have inquired of God and received a revelation of what you can become, you have a place to focus your faith. Be solid and fearless in what the Lord has revealed to you and He will bring it to pass. He says you will live by His faith.

God is your source! You have no ability to bring the revelation to pass, so don't worry about how your revelation will happen. God is fully aware that it's impossible for you. Even though you have no proof, your faithfulness and commitment to Him assure the manifestation of the revelation. Believe steadfastly in God's ability and keep seeking Him first, *"so that your faith might not rest on men's wisdom, but on God's power"* (1 Corinthians 2:5).

Not that we are competent in ourselves to claim anything for ourselves, but our competence comes from God (2 Corinthians 3:5).

Suddenly, you can do everything through Him who gives you strength. (See Philippians 4:13.) Remember what was said before:

- It wasn't Peter's ability that caught the fish, but God's ability. (See John 21:6.)
- It wasn't human ability that fed the 5,000, but God's ability. (See Luke 9:13-17.)
- It wasn't human ability at Jericho, but God's ability. (See Hebrews 11:30.)
- It won't be your ability either.

With God as your ultimate source, you can reach greater and higher heights. With God, all things are possible and your limitations vanish in the light of His ability.

Remember when Peter walked on water? As long as he stayed focused on Jesus standing on the water, he remained within the miraculous. As soon as he looked around at the waves and wind, however, he began to sink. Why did Peter doubt?

In time, after putting into practice the principles we've studied, you will get tired of doubt and fear. You'll realize that they lead you nowhere. Just like Peter, you'll decide that you want the truth and nothing but the truth. You'll want to seize God's revelation of what you can become. You'll decide you want God's best for your life, even if it means losing close friends, family, or life's comforts. You'll set your mind to gain understanding and humble yourself before God. You'll determine that you won't go back, but will move straightforward into your revelation and achieve your divine potential.

Once the Word of God is rooted in you and you're communicating with God in prayer, you are carried along by the Spirit of God, fully aware that the revelation from God is beyond your natural capabilities. You rely solely on God and His ability to move you forward. You are armed with the revelation of what you can become and confident in God's ability to accomplish it for you.

> *You will not fear the terror of night, nor the arrow that flies by day, nor the pestilence that stalks in the darkness, nor the plague that destroys at midday. A thousand may fall at your side, ten thousand at your right hand, but it will not come near you* (Psalm 91:5-7).

> *No harm will befall you, no disaster will come near your tent. For he will command his angels concerning you to guard you in all your ways; they will lift you up in their hands, so that you will not strike your foot against a stone. You will tread upon the lion and the cobra; you will trample the great lion and the serpent* (Psalm 91:10-13).

YOUR DIVINE POTENTIAL POWER POINTS

1. Seek God for revelation through prayer.
2. Write the revelation down.
3. Begin development of your plan.
4. Start your journal.
5. Overcome and conquer unbelief.

Write a prayer asking God to control your flesh and fill you with the desire to pray.

_____

_____

_____

_____

Now thank God for filling you with His faith to do the impossible.

CHAPTER 8

Performance Principle Number Four

Take Action to Achieve Your Divine Potential

Experiencing the Power of God

Failure to plan as God dictates and then to take action is the reason why many Christians don't seize God's potential for their lives. Many quit upon getting a revelation. They just talk about the revelation: "One day I'll be this or that," but they never take action to bring it to pass. They are waiting for God to do it for them. They have come all the way to the Promised Land, but are not willing to take the action necessary to enter in and bring the revelation to pass. There is still work to be done.

Make up your mind to work through God's plan in His timing and in His way. Meditate now on these promises from God's Word:

> *The soul of a lazy man desires, and has nothing; But the soul of the diligent shall be made rich* (Proverbs 13:4, NKJV).

> *The plans of the diligent lead surely to plenty, But those of everyone who is hasty, surely to poverty* (Proverbs 21:5, NKJV).

Don't try to do things your own way. You received a revelation and are understandably eager to get moving. However, if you don't take the time to plan as God dictates, it'll take much longer and you'll encounter many more trials than are necessary. If you do things your way, and try to make them happen in your time, you may become frustrated and discouraged, and be tempted to quit. You might even blame God and turn into a negative, bitter person.

My Story—Failure to Obey

As a six-year-old child, I distinctly remember hearing the Lord speak to me and reveal what He wanted me to become. I remember the day as clearly as yesterday. My mother, my sister, and I were visiting with our cousins in St. Louis, Missouri. One afternoon, I was playing in the yard with my cousins. There was a slight incline from the sidewalk up to my aunt's house with a row of hedges separating the sidewalk from her yard. My cousins, sister, and I were playing, taking turns rolling down the incline from the top of the hill down to the hedges.

After rolling down the hill numerous times, I was distracted by what appeared to me to be an unusual color in the sky. The sun's rays pierced through the clouds, highlighting them as though they were three-dimensional and generating what seemed like a rainbow of colors.

I remember lying on my back, looking up and feeling a sense of awe and wonderment about God. Then almost instantaneously, I became unaware of the sound of the other children playing, the birds in the trees, and the cars passing by. It was as though someone had turned down the sound of the world around me. Then the silence was broken and I heard a voice say, *"I want you to be a preacher, a teacher of my Word."*

I don't know how long I lay there, but I do know that the voice I heard was the voice of God. He was revealing to me what He wanted me to become. I got up and ran into the house, calling out to everyone that God had called me to be a preacher. I don't know what others thought about what I said, but it was with certain determination from that point on that I knew what my life was supposed to be about and what I was to become.

When I entered first grade, the teacher asked us all what we intended to be when we grew up. I remember confessing that I was going to be a preacher. She then took a piece of paper and taped underneath each of our desks the title of what we were going to become. For a period of time I was known as Reverend Lowe. Other students were also known by what they had planned to be when they grew up: Dr. Steel, Nurse Rivers, mechanic Jones, airplane pilot Williams, and many other titles.

My father was the principal of my elementary school, and on one of his visits to our classroom, he noticed that I was labeled as Reverend Lowe. He said nothing at the time, but when we got home, he asked me why I was called Reverend Lowe. I told him it was because God told me to be a preacher. I remember his telling me that God did not want me to be a preacher, but to be a doctor. God wanted me to be somebody who would make money and help other people.

As one of three children, I assumed that my father knew more about what God wanted for me than I did. From that day forward, I decided I would be a doctor. Whenever I was asked, I would tell everyone that I planned to be a doctor.

In the sixth grade, I took my first health course. For some reason, although I had been an A-B student, I was unable to make As or Bs in health. Instead, I made Cs. It was a great disappointment. At the same time, I began to feel uneasy about becoming a doctor. I began to question whether this was indeed what God wanted for me.

I spent an uneasy summer between the seventh and eighth grades. I was troubled that God wanted me to be a preacher and not a doctor. I struggled with the issue and finally concluded that I was to be a doctor. Then in the summer before the ninth grade, I remember spending many hours alone, feeling uncomfortable about my chosen career for life. I remember many hours when many tears rolled down my face, and how I was feeling lost and uncertain about who I was and what I was to become.

I used to sit by myself, pondering. What was life about? Did it have any purpose? Why was I born? Why was there so much suffering in the world? Why was there death? Why were children born handicapped? Time and time again, I felt strongly that God wanted me to be a preacher. And time and time again, I remembered that my father had told me that God wanted me to be a doctor. I was supposed to be a doctor, yet it didn't feel right.

Throughout high school, I took all the science and math courses I could, with the intent and purpose of going to medical school. It was not until my senior year that I realized I was not happy with the thought of becoming a doctor. I kept hearing a voice say, "*I want you to be a preacher.*" Finally, I asked God (or whoever the voice was) to leave me alone. I asked Him to let me be what I wanted to be.

I knew I was musically inclined and decided I wanted to be a musician. I played all the instruments in the band and could write music. Certainly, God had created me to be a musician.

I went off to college to become a musician. Then, after recognizing that basically a major in music would only make me a teacher, I decided I might need to major in something that would get me some money. I looked over my options. I decided that I would major in either music or business. Then I prayed and asked God which one He wanted me to major in. I remember hearing Him say, "*You will not be happy until you do what I say.*" To this day, I remember the anger that I felt against God. I told him again, "Leave me alone!" I don't remember His response. In fact, I don't think He had one.

I decided I would major in business with a minor in music. In this way I would be sure of making money and doing what I enjoyed for myself. Indeed, when I finished college, I was able to find a good job and made good money. However, I was not happy. I dreaded going to work every day. I hated my job. The money was good, but it did not buy my happiness. I remember my father telling me to just think about my paycheck; it would make me feel better about my job. No, it did not!

After a year and a half, I quit. I decided I would pursue music. I became a music producer and songwriter. I worked with various R&B groups. I was finally doing what made me happy. However, I didn't make the money that I made in my 8-to-5 job. This was fine for a while, but never being sure about my income or that I could place another song with another group made me uncomfortable. I grew weary of the constant effort of trying to make a living.

One late evening as I was sitting at the piano, writing a song, I heard the Lord say to me, "*What are you doing?*"

I told Him that I was writing the song.

He asked me, *"What for?"*

I told him so that I could make a living.

He then asked, *"What for?"*

I said, "So that I could survive."

Again, He asked *"What for?"*

And then it happened. I realized that there was no purpose to what I was doing. I was incomplete. I had no reason for existing. That night, about one o'clock in the morning, I gave up. I told the Lord, whatever He wanted me to be, I would be. I would accept the call into the ministry. The burden was lifted. I felt peace for the first time in a long time.

The Lord led me step by step, and with each step of the way, I found peace and joy. It didn't matter what job I worked at, I had yielded myself to do and to become whatever He wanted. All He had to do was make it clear to me and I would do it. I asked Him to open the doors to the way in which He wanted me to go. If a direction or an action was not in accordance with His will, all He had to do was make it clear to me and I would change it.

The only thing I would not do for the Lord was become a pastor! I didn't mind assisting other pastors, but I never wanted to pastor myself. I was content with being a minister of music and ministering to people through music. I was assisting the pastor of a fifteen-member church when the pastor informed me that he was going to leave town. He told me the church would be mine while he was gone. I told him I didn't want the church. I was not going to be a pastor. He told me he was going to leave and I was going to be the pastor.

Sure enough, he didn't show up the next week. Reluctantly, I conducted the services for four weeks. After the fourth week, the pastor returned and permanently resigned. The congregation asked me to take his place. I told them I was not a pastor and would only shepherd them until they could find somebody else or unless God clearly said otherwise.

Six months later, the congregation had grown to seventy-five members! The congregation and I concluded that it was God's will for my life to be a pastor.

Now, after over twenty years of being a pastor, I know for a certainty that God called me when I was six and told me what I was to become, but for twenty years I refused to obey His will. For another ten years, I refused to ultimately submit to His perfect will. But I can genuinely tell you now that I wish I had given up sooner. I will accept nothing for my life other than shepherding God's people. Life has purpose for me now. Life has meaning. In all things I have joy and peace. I have submitted myself to becoming what God wants me to be. I have learned that the created one is content when he has become what he was created for.

Boldly Go Where Others Fear to Tread

Many people have lived their lives, doing things they were never meant to do, and experiencing discouragement, dissatisfaction, and emptiness even after having done a job well. Just like me, they may have spent many years in school, studying to be what they have become, but still they find themselves unfulfilled. Instead of finding joy and ease at what they do, they find themselves stressed and reluctant to face each day.

Many move from job to job and from career to career in never-ending quests, trying to find true happiness in life. Sadly, some will experience a measure of success and be well thought of by others, but deep down inside, they feel incomplete. What are they doing wrong? They simply fail to work at becoming what God had designed them to be.

This will not be you! We are going to take action on the plan of God to achieve your divine potential.

What good is it, my brothers, if a man claims to have faith but has no deeds? Can such faith save him? (James 2:14)

Now it is time to act upon all the Word you've heard and learned. Your divine potential awaits you. There is no weapon formed against you that can prosper and prevent you from achieving God's purposes in your life. Now you have been endued with the power of God to accomplish what He has revealed to you. You have faith based upon the Word. You have aligned yourself with that Word, thereby qualifying yourself to achieve your potential. You have asked God what your potential is, and you have developed a plan to follow. Now you boldly take the necessary action to achieve your divine potential.

Discipline your mind to not accept the status quo anymore; dare to dream and see visions. If you're able to conceive it, you are able to achieve it. Remember, man cannot create anything. The very fact of your ability to conceive a thing in a dream or a vision is the reality of God creating the thought in you. His Word states that He will give you the desires of your heart. He will not give you a dream that you can't achieve. If it is in you, you can do it. Remember His words to Joshua:

> *Be strong and courageous, because you will lead these people to inherit the land I swore to their forefathers to give them. Be strong and very courageous. Be careful to obey all the law my servant Moses gave you; do not turn from it to the right or to the left, that you may be successful wherever you go. Do not let this Book of the Law depart from your mouth; meditate on it day and night, so that you may be careful to do everything written in it. Then you will be prosperous and successful. Have I not commanded you? Be strong and courageous. Do not be terrified; do not be discouraged, for the Lord your God will be with you wherever you go* (Joshua 1:6-9).

These may very well become your words. You know your mission in life now. Therefore, as God commanded Joshua, you also are commanded to be bold and courageous so that you may be a blessing to your generation. The enemy will still come against you, but he will flee from you when you stand your ground and proclaim who you are and in whose name you have come. When you act in faith in God's Word, God acts on your behalf and things happen. Great things occur in life because someone is willing to be bold and courageous enough to go beyond normal expectations. You have divine potential. You are able to take bold and courageous action that will bring about changes in your generation that will be a blessing to people around you—and possibly the whole world.

You Can't Advance by Remaining Where You Are

So many gathered that there was no room left, not even outside the door, and he preached the word to them. Some men came, bringing to him a paralytic, carried by four of them. Since they could not get him to Jesus because of the crowd, they made an opening in the roof above Jesus and, after digging through it, lowered the mat the paralyzed man was lying on. When Jesus saw their faith, he said to the paralytic, "Son, your sins are forgiven." Now some teachers of the law were sitting there, thinking to themselves, "Why does this fellow talk like that? He's blaspheming! Who can forgive sins but God alone?" Immediately Jesus knew in his spirit that this was what they were thinking in their hearts, and he said to them, "Why are you thinking these things? Which is easier: to say to the paralytic, 'Your sins are forgiven,' or to say, 'Get up, take your mat and walk'? But that you may know that the Son of Man has authority on earth to forgive sins . . . ." He said to the paralytic, "I tell you, get up, take your mat and go home." He got up, took his mat and walked out in full view of them all. This amazed everyone and they praised God, saying, "We have never seen anything like this!" (Mark 2:2-12)

See what bold actions they took. They believed that Jesus could heal their friend, and they took steps to see that what they believed would come to pass. They dug a hole through the roof and lowered their friend down to Jesus. How did Jesus react to the actions of these men? Faith exemplified itself by their action. It caused Jesus to act for their benefit.

When you believe in a thing strongly enough, you will not accept "No" for an answer. You will do whatever is necessary to bring it to pass. With the knowledge you have, "No" is merely a river you have to cross. You will find a way to cross it. Look for the bridge, build one, make a raft, swim it, jump over it, create a dam, and when necessary, part the waters. You will find a way around "No." When God is for you, "No" cannot be against you.

When you are grounded in the Word, having aligned yourself with it, and inquired of God about your potential, then when you act, things always happen. God guarantees it! He does not do things that we should do ourselves. Remember, we are partners and co-workers with God. We do our part and He does His part. Too many are waiting on God to move when it is their move. An encouraging word is found here: *"Therefore, my dear brothers, stand firm. Let nothing move you. Always give yourselves fully to the work of the Lord, because you know that your labor in the Lord is not in vain"* (1 Corinthians 15:58).

Work With What You Have and God Will Give You More

Matthew 25:23-30 explains that if *"you have been faithful with a few things,"* God will refer to you as a *"good and faithful servant,"* and He *"will put you in charge of many things."* On the other hand, if you're afraid and do nothing with your talents, God refers to you as a *"wicked, lazy servant!"* and takes away your talent, giving it to the faithful servants. To everyone who is faithful with little, God gives more in abundance. Let that be *you.*

God is obligated by His Word to give you the tools and resources necessary to move you to the next level of growth when you prove yourself faithful at your current level. The Lord gives to each of us "according to his ability." In one of Jesus' parables, the master gave each of his servants talents to see what they would do with them. The servant with the five talents took action immediately and gained five more. The servant with the two talents also took action immediately and gained two more. The third servant didn't multiply his talents. When the master returned, he gave more talents to the two men who took action with what they had.

> *Whatever you do, work at it with all your heart, as working for the Lord, not for men, since you know that you will receive an inheritance from the Lord as a reward. It is the Lord Christ you are serving* (Colossians 3:23-24).

- If you can bake good cookies, then bake! Remember Famous Amos!
- If you can cook delicious chicken, then cook! Remember Colonel Sanders!
- If you can program a computer, then program! Remember Bill Gates!

Whatever talent or skill you have, *use it* and God will reward you for your faithfulness with increase. No matter what you lack, God will provide it. That is His Word. That is His will.

Don't Let Negative Circumstances Discourage You

The Spirit of God is always there to lead you into truth and deliver you out of your current situation. Don't allow circumstances to change you. Instead, make plans to change your circumstances. Begin by thanking God for the journey He has mapped out for you.

In Genesis 29-31, we read about Jacob's interesting journey, which led him to his relative Laban's house. Here Jacob endured many negative circumstances before God's plan was clearly revealed to him.

- Jacob worked for seven years for Laban's daughter Rachel; then Laban deceived Jacob into marrying Leah.
- Jacob worked another seven years for Laban in order to marry Rachel.
- Along the way, Laban cheated Jacob and changed his wages ten times.
- After all this, Jacob had nothing to show for his hard labor except for his wives and children. At this point, he asked Laban's permission to leave for his own homeland.
- Laban pleaded with Jacob to stay, offering wages of his choice. Laban realized his livestock had increased greatly under Jacob's care.

After viewing all of Jacob's negative circumstances, one might wonder, "Where was God in all this?" What God did for Jacob, He will do for you also. Let's look!

- God stayed with Jacob and never left his side. *Jehovah-Rohi* is your Shepherd.
- God protected Jacob from any harm. *Jehovah-Shammah* is your ever-present help in times of need.
- God blessed everything Jacob put his hands to do. *Jehovah-Jireh* is your Provider.
- God continually observed all of Laban's deceitfulness concerning Jacob. God had a plan not yet revealed to Jacob. God is the Great *I AM* and there's nothing too big for God to handle.

Now for the rest of the story: Finally in a dream, God gave Jacob His plan on how to achieve his divine potential and prosper. God revealed to Jacob how to successfully increase the inferior livestock: the spotted or speckled ones. So when Laban asked Jacob to choose his wages, Jacob chose the inferior livestock, as God had instructed.

Jacob was instructed to take branches and peel the bark in lines to expose the white underneath and create stripes on the branches. Jacob was then to put the striped branches in the watering troughs in front of the stronger female cows when they were in heat. Somehow these females would know to mate near the branches. Jacob's stronger animals would reproduce speckled and striped offspring, leaving the weaker cattle to Laban. God's plan for Jacob seemed foolish and implausible. But look at the results.

Remember, nothing is impossible for God. God will give you a plan for reaching the point He wants you to reach. He will give you the strength to get there. God always has a plan for you to overcome your circumstances. Listen to Him. Take action according to what He tells you. He's committed to your success!

We have another story the Lord has given to us when everything seems to be against us, and we need encouragement to keep pressing on without looking back. After the Hebrews had left Egypt, Pharaoh changed his mind and marched out after them.

> *As Pharaoh approached, the Israelites looked up, and there were the Egyptians, marching after them. They were terrified and cried out to the Lord. They said to Moses, "Was it because there were no graves in Egypt that you brought us to the desert to die? What have you done to us by bringing us out of Egypt? Didn't we say to you in Egypt, 'Leave us alone; let us serve the Egyptians'? It would have been better for us to serve the Egyptians than to die in the desert!" Moses answered the people, "Do not be afraid. Stand firm and you will see the deliverance the Lord will bring you today. The Egyptians you see today you will never see again. The Lord will fight for you; you need only to be still"* (Exodus 14:10-14).

Here we see the results of the lack of faith on the part of the people. They were terrified. They cried out with words of unbelief. They wanted to give up. What caused their fear? They looked up and saw the Egyptians approaching. This tells us that we must be careful in our quest for our divine potential: when we see trouble, we must not fear. We must do what Moses told them to do: stand firm in faith with nothing wavering. Then, he tells them the second thing. He tells them to see the deliverance of the Lord, take their eyes off the object of fear, and place them on the Lord.

Moses was teaching them to see in the supernatural. They were seeing in the natural, but not perceiving. They were looking, but not observing. We must learn to see with a discerning eye, to see things as they *really* are so that we may have peace in the midst of the storm. We must see God. We walk by faith, not by sight.

If we walk by sight in the natural, we will fail. The natural is filled with challenges that threaten to undermine our faith and confidence in the Lord. The people saw the Red Sea and Pharaoh's army, and it brought about fear and doubt. Then, as the people were crying out, the Lord asked an unusual question and gave a specific order that speaks volumes to us.

> *The Lord said to Moses, "Why are you crying out to me? Tell the Israelites to move on. Raise your staff and stretch*

out your hand over the sea to divide the water so that the Israelites can go through the sea on dry ground" (Exodus 14:15-16).

In other words, God was saying, "You have heard my instructions. I am with you. There is no need for you to cry out to me. This is not a time for prayer. Get moving. Take action. I told you to take them to the Promised Land. Now raise your staff and divide the water. Do the impossible."

The important thing to recognize here is that if the sea were going to part, it would require the people and Moses to act boldly before God acted. They had to move forward and Moses had to raise his staff.

If we have heard from God, then any obstacle in our way is not there to stop us. It is simply there to strengthen us as we see the deliverance of the Lord. We must take bold action. We have been given the power of His presence with us. Therefore we can say:

The Lord is my light and my salvation—whom shall I fear? The Lord is the stronghold of my life—of whom shall I be afraid? When evil men advance against me to devour my flesh, when my enemies and my foes attack me, they will stumble and fall. Though an army besiege me, my heart will not fear; though war break out against me, even then will I be confident (Psalm 27:1-3).

You have the ability to take bold, courageous action! You have developed your faith and are now more familiar with the Word. The Word has strengthened your faith, and if you have the faith of a mustard seed, you can say to the mountain, "Be removed," and it will be removed. The power you have is of God and it is in your hands. Don't hold back; give it all you've got. God will act when your faith comes alive. You have the Master of the universe behind you. You can be bold and unafraid of your circumstances. Therefore, take action and subdue your adversaries, which are fear and lack of faith! You've got the victory!

Another powerful encouragement for us to take action is found in the way David fought Goliath. The Bible says, *"As the Philistine moved closer to attack him, David ran quickly toward the battle line to meet him"* (1 Samuel 17:48). He took bold action; it is for us to do the same with regard to everything we set our hand to do.

Now consider—what if:

- Noah had not built the ark?
- Moses had just prayed for the deliverance of the Israelites?
- Joshua had not gone around the walls?
- David had not fought Goliath?
- Jesus had not gone to the cross?

God has given you His word that He is with you. Do not be afraid to take action.

You Will Do the Impossible With God!

- Submit to God's plan each day.
- Take action on God's plan.
- "Just Do It!"

YOUR DIVINE POTENTIAL POWER POINTS

1. God has powerful plans for you to implement.
2. Don't do things your way. Pursue God's way.
3. Don't be discouraged by negative circumstances. Always be encouraged.

4. With God, seize your divine potential and accomplish the impossible.

Write down the plan(s) that God is giving you.
Write down the steps you'll take now to implement what God wants for you.

⟫⟫⟫⟪⟪⟪

Write a prayer asking God for wisdom and perseverance to implement His plans:

_____

_____

_____

_____

_____

_____

_____

_____

CHAPTER 9

Performance Principle Number Five

Hold Out and Be Diligently Patient!

Don't Quit! Seize Your Divine Potential

You have come a long way. You know that you have divine potential. Now, you have been given the tools to develop into what God originally designed you to be. You have learned and done these things:

- You have been given a source of endless empowerment.
- You have been given divine directives from God.
- You have learned how to verbalize and visualize.
- You have learned how to meditate, apply, and perform.
- You have found out who you are.
- You have learned to align yourself with the Word of God.
- You have inquired from God about your divine potential.
- You have taken action to achieve your divine potential.

Now God gives us the one additional thing we need to add to our faith in order to assure our development to seize our divine potential.

The Dynamic Duo

> *We want each of you to show this same* **diligence** *to the very end, in order to make your hope sure. We do not want you to become lazy, but to imitate those who through faith and* **patience** *inherit what has been promised* (Hebrews 6:11-12, emphasis mine).

There are two words I would like to emphasize in this scripture: *diligence* and *patience*. *Diligence* also means *persistence*. Because I like the force and the power of these two similar words when they're put together, I will sometimes use the term "persistently diligent" to emphasize the attitude we must have in order to accomplish what God has given us to do. There will always be opposition to the work of the Lord in the earth, but if we are "persistently diligent," we have the power of God working with us to bring to pass what He has commanded us to do.

Patient means "able to endure; capable of waiting." The Bible is full of scriptures that talk about waiting on the Lord. This is one thing you must learn. In order to receive from God you must understand that God's timing probably is not the same as yours. If He gives you something to accomplish, it may not occur when you think it should, but it will occur when He has designed for it to happen. Often God will not allow things to happen when you think they should just to prove that He is still in charge.

If we are persistently diligent and patient, the scripture says that we inherit, not that we *will* inherit, what has been promised. Victory will come to you when you are diligent and patient in waiting on God. You must learn to hold out. You win when you continue to press on without giving up.

I like to put it this way: we should be "diligently patient." When you have faith and you are "diligently patient" to keep pressing on faithfully, your faith ultimately overcomes any irresistible force. How many of us have given up on God simply because things did not happen as quickly as we desired? We must learn to hold out! He knows the right time to allow you to have the victory. Remember the old saying: "He might not come when you want Him, but He's right on time!"

Be still before the Lord and wait patiently for him; do not fret when men succeed in their ways, when they carry out their wicked schemes (Psalm 37:7).

Wait for the Lord and keep his way. He will exalt you to inherit the land; when the wicked are cut off, you will see it (Psalm 37:34).

God will test you and your willingness to wait on Him. You are not alone in your waiting on God's deliverance:

- Noah waited 100 years while building the ark before the flood came.
- Abraham waited twenty-five years for his promised son and showed his trust in God by his actions. He lived in tents because he was expecting a permanent place to be provided by God.
- Jacob was diligently patient and served Laban for more than fifteen years before he was freed.
- Joseph waited over thirteen years before his dream was fulfilled.
- Israel waited in Egypt over 300 years.
- Moses waited in the desert forty years before God used him.
- David had to wait until Saul died before he could become king
- Paul waited thirteen years before his ministry was completely launched.

Follow the examples of these great acts of faith by men who persevered, never giving up, until they received what God said was for them.

Abraham

> When God made his promise to Abraham, since there was no one greater for him to swear by, he swore by himself, saying, "I will surely bless you and give you many descendants." And so after waiting patiently, Abraham received what was promised (Hebrews 6:13-15).

He waited for twenty-five years, calling himself "Exalted Father," and he had no children. And while he waited, he experienced hardship and trouble with:

- His father slowing him down
- Kings desiring his wife
- Famine and war
- Family disorder and other problems with his relatives
- A dysfunctional family with two wives at each other's throats
- Years of silence from God after the promise was made many years before

Yet the Bible says of him, he believed God and God judged him righteous for believing. He believed and he waited. He held out until God's promises came to pass.

Moses

> By faith Moses, when he had grown up, refused to be known as the son of Pharaoh's daughter. He chose to be mistreated along with the people of God rather than to enjoy the pleasures of sin for a short time. He regarded disgrace for the sake of Christ as of greater value than the treasures of Egypt, because he was looking ahead to his reward. By faith he left Egypt, not fearing the king's anger; he persevered because he saw him who is invisible (Hebrews 11:24-27).

Here is a man who had it all, but realized God offered him more. He lived to fulfill his divine potential. Like many of us, he was not ready in the beginning. But over time, God led him one step after another. He became the great prophet that we know today. He endured and held out for forty years. He was diligently patient, trusting, and believing God.

David

He waited for the kingdom that was promised to him when he was a young lad. He fought for the nation and served in the army, fighting Israel's enemies. He spent year after year being hunted and running for his life. Yet he continued to believe God. Even when he had the opportunity to kill King Saul, he did not disrespect God's anointed man. Even after King Saul's death, it took him awhile before he became king over the nation. He waited until God's time. Yet all the while, he was diligently patient, waiting on God.

Now, if these imperfect people—Abraham, Moses, and David—could receive the promises of God, how much more are we certain to receive, having the righteousness of God in Christ? Notice, they remained persistently diligent to accomplish God's plan even when things didn't go their way. How are you when things don't go the way you want? Do you get angry? Do you blame others? What happens in your church when the pastor doesn't do what you want him to do? Do you quit the church? Do you talk about him? If so, stop! When things don't go the way you want them to go, make sure you remain persistently diligent to God's plan.

God desires for you to achieve your divine potential. He has a plan for your life and wants to fulfill that plan. Every challenge has come to strengthen you and prepare you to achieve your divine potential. Therefore, hold fast to your confidence. If you fall down, don't give up. Get up! Press on!

Remember these words of the prophet Micah: *"Do not gloat over me, my enemy! Though I have fallen, I will rise. Though I sit in darkness, the Lord will be my light"* (Micah 7:8).

He knew his victory would come to pass. But he also reveals to us that there will be times when we will fall down. Don't let such times discourage you. These things must be. With God, you have the absolute certainty that you will be victorious. It is only a question of time. Though the true reality of the revelation may wait, do not lose confidence. God says, *"For the revelation awaits an appointed time; it speaks of the end and will not prove false. Though it linger, wait for it; it will certainly come and will not delay"* (Habakkuk 2:3).

Did you get that? There is an appointed time for the revelation to occur. That's why the scripture also tells us, *"Let us not become weary in doing good, for at the proper time we will reap a harvest if we do not give up"* (Galatians 6:9). Don't give up! Your time is coming. Just remain diligently patient. Good things come to those who wait. This is profoundly true for those who wait on the Lord.

Focus on What Is *"IN"* You, Not What Is *"ON"* You

Remember, in the process of waiting, you may have trials, but these trials cannot overcome you. You have the ability to overcome them. You have been given a divine directive to subdue and take dominion over them. Therefore, let not your heart be troubled. (See John 14:1.)

Trials can be either stumbling blocks or stepping-stones. They're stumbling blocks if you do not address them in the right way. They are there for you to fall *down*. They're stepping-stones when you realize you have victory over them. They are there for you to rise up. Either way, satan means them for bad. With your confidence in God, He will make them for good.

How you handle your trials depends on your attitude. Consider two people on the same job. One considers it hell. He or she is always complaining and finding fault about the job. Another considers it a blessing. He or she is always commenting about how he or she enjoys it. They both do the same work. What makes the difference? Attitude.

You can now have a great attitude about everything you face in life. You have the certainty that God works everything out together for your good. Hold your head up. If it hasn't happened yet, it will happen soon. Take this attitude: I will see my blessing today. If what you have been praying for has not occurred by this evening, start confessing I will see my blessing tomorrow. When tomorrow comes, start over. I will see my blessing today. It is all about attitude. Your attitude is great, because your God is great.

Consider now the life of Paul. He was another person who went through many trials but diligently and patiently waited on the Lord:

> *I have worked much harder, been in prison more frequently, been flogged more severely, and been exposed to death again and again. Five times I received from the Jews the forty lashes minus one. Three times I was beaten with rods, once I was stoned, three times I was shipwrecked, I spent a night and a day in the open sea, I have been constantly on the move. I have been in danger from rivers, in danger from bandits, in danger from my own countrymen, in danger from Gentiles; in danger in the city, in danger in the country, in danger at sea; and in danger from false brothers. I have labored and toiled and have often gone without sleep; I have known hunger and thirst and have often gone without food; I have been cold and naked. Besides everything else, I face daily the pressure of my concern for all the churches. Who is weak, and I do not feel weak? Who is led into sin, and I do not inwardly burn?* (2 Corinthians 11:23-29)

See how much he went through, but he never lost the faith. He stated that even when he was suffering, *"I consider that our present sufferings are not worth comparing with the glory that will be revealed in us"* (Romans 8:18). In order to be strong he also said, *"One thing I do: Forgetting what is behind and straining toward what is ahead, I press on toward the goal to win the prize for which God has called me heavenward in Christ Jesus"* (Philippians 3:13-14).

He kept his eyes on the prize. Paul clearly understood that if he took his eyes off of Jesus or all of that which he had been called to, he would become discouraged and despondent. Because you have been invested with divine potential, you should focus on that which is *in* you rather than that which is *on* you.

Finally, when he'd come to the end of his life, he had this to say: *"I have fought the good fight, I have finished the race, I have kept the faith. Now there is in store for me the crown of righteousness, which the Lord, the righteous Judge, will award to me on that day—*

and not only to me, but also to all who have longed for his appearing" (2 Timothy 4:7-8).

See, he speaks for us also. We must keep our eyes on the prize. Remember, if we look at our circumstances, we will falter. The risk is that we might lose faith and miss our divine potential. Do not allow struggles to tempt you to abort the work that God has begun in you. Your circumstances don't affect your divine potential.

There is so much to be said about struggles and trials. The Word of God constantly gives us encouragement to help us know that we can make it through. In every encounter we have, God is with us.

Let this confidence be in you: " ... *that in all things God works for the good of those who love him, who have been called according to his purpose"* (Romans 8:28). You have been called to His purpose and to mature to your divine potential. The trials you face are merely trials to strengthen you.

> *Consider it pure joy, my brothers, whenever you face trials of many kinds, because you know that the testing of your faith develops perseverance. Perseverance must finish its work so that you may be mature and complete, not lacking anything* (James 1:2-4).

Trials are a part of your growth, and they are necessary for your development. You can rejoice in every trial, because you can be certain that God is with you. He will never leave you or forsake you. He has not brought you this far to desert you. He who has begun this work in you will see it through to completion.

Again, let not your heart be troubled, for you have been called by God. You have been ordained by God. You have been anointed by God to fulfill your divine potential. This is absolutely certain about your life. If you do not give up, you will reap a harvest that will astound you!

Three Things Being Persistently Diligent and Patient Will Do for You

1. They will give you power in all areas of life.

Diligent hands will rule, but laziness ends in slave labor (Proverbs 12:24).

Do you see a man skilled in his work? He will serve before kings; he will not serve before obscure men (Proverbs 22:29).

2. They will lead you to prosperity.

Lazy hands make a man poor, but diligent hands bring wealth (Proverbs 10:4).

3. They will lead you to abundant life.

The plans of the diligent lead to profit as surely as haste leads to poverty (Proverbs 21:5).

The sluggard craves and gets nothing, but the desires of the diligent are fully satisfied (Proverbs 13:4).

And without faith it is impossible to please God, because anyone who comes to him must believe that he exists and that he rewards those who earnestly seek him (Hebrews 11:6).

What you will become isn't dependent on what you have now, but upon how you use it!
Remember how God tested and prepared David in private. As a young boy, David first proved himself to be a faithful servant by keeping his father's sheep. Alone in the pasture where he could have run away, he defeated a bear and a lion, proving himself faithful at defending his father's flock.

There are similar battles in your life: bears and lions you need to overcome. Don't run away in fear. Instead say, "Bring 'em on!" God gives you the little things first to prepare you to take on the greater things! David conquered many personal trials that were all necessary to prepare him for conquering a giant a little later in his life.

Consider how he had victory:

- Over the **spirit of pride** by doing the lowly job of tending sheep, even after coming and going in Saul's court—and already being anointed king.
- Over the **spirit of disobedience** to his father—to be a servant and deliver his brothers' food on the battlefield.
- Over the **spirit of slothfulness** to do the will of his father— he quickly did as he asked.
- Over his brother and the **spirit of anger**—when he challenged him.
- Over the **spirit of unbelief** in others—when they made fun of him.
- Over **conforming to the world's way**—when he refused to wear Saul's armor.

Stop focusing on the giants in your life—those things you can't control or change. Realize that the reason you haven't been able to defeat the giant you face today is that you haven't yet defeated the bear and the lion that confronted you yesterday. You have to prove yourself faithful in the little things, and in time, God will make you ruler over those giant things!

Remember: *"No temptation has seized you except what is common to man"* (1 Corinthians 10:13). God has already provided a way out for you! Your human weaknesses are neither problems for God nor have they caught God off guard. He already has a solution to meet your needs right where you are. So be persistently diligent!

Don't let your current circumstances discourage you from achieving your potential:

1. Since life is more than your physical existence, the true measure of success isn't limited to physical observation.

2. Your divine potential is, therefore, more than your physical existence and it extends into eternity.

3. What may seem small in this life can equate to greatness in the world to come.

Again, be persistently diligent!

As you are faithful to God, God is faithful to you, forming a powerful cycle that manifests in your life. As you watch His faithfulness in your life, this builds your trust in Him. Trusting in Him increases your faith to greater levels. God then rewards your faithfulness with a few more things. If you are faithful with those things, He will give you more. If you again are faithful with that little more, He will give you even more. And so on to even greater levels of faith until there is no mountain, no giant, and no problem too big for you to overcome.

"Moreover it is required in stewards, that a man be found faithful" (1 Corinthians 4:2, KJV).

Success in life is not required by God, but faithfulness is! Now know this: faithfulness to God will always produce success! Jesus said:

Therefore consider carefully how you listen. Whoever has will be given **more***; whoever does not have, even what he thinks he has will be taken from him* (Luke 8:18, emphasis mine).

Here is one of the greatest revelations ever given by Jesus to assure your success in achieving your divine potential.

Let us note that He spoke these words to those disciples who were faithfully following Him. He told them that because of their faithfulness, He would reveal to them the secrets of the Kingdom of God. This knowledge was the revelation of the things of God that would be given so that they would be productive in their lives.

These words were spoken after He had given them the Parable of the Sower. (See Luke 8:11-15.) This parable shows that the Word of God gives us the ability to achieve our divine potential in life. It also details the various distractions that hinder us from achieving it. The final result is true productivity and success in life.

He speaks of those who retain the Word and by persevering, produce a crop. Consider now the magnitude of all that can be done. One simple seed, one simple revelation heard from God, has within it the ability to produce a crop that will have more seed to produce a greater crop. Let us bear in mind that it is God's will for us to live life abundantly. Abundant living comes about from our faithful commitment to the Word of God.

- In the parable, the seed is the Word of God. It gives you the power to achieve your divine potential. It is the force that launches you to greatness.
- Those along the path are the ones who hear, and then the devil comes and takes away the Word from their hearts, so that they may not believe and be saved.
- Those on the rock are the ones who receive the Word with joy when they hear it, but they have no root. They believe for a while, but in the time of testing they fall away and fail to accomplish much.
- The seed that fell among thorns stands for those who hear, but as they go on their way, they are choked by life's worries, riches, and pleasures, and they don't mature as God would desire for them.
- But the seed on good soil stands for those with noble and good hearts, who hear the Word, retain it, and by persevering produce a crop.

Faithfully listen to the Word of God—your seed. Jesus said that the farmer does not know how the seed grows nor does he concern himself with how. He just plants it in fertile soil and God does the rest. So let it be with you. Let the Word be planted in you and God will cause it to blossom.

- Let the Word be planted deep in your heart—literally "take it to heart."
- Listen with your whole being.
  - Understand the Word of God and do it.
- When testing comes, take hold of the Word and don't depart from it.
  - Believe it and keep doing it, no matter what.
- Clean all thorns out of your heart.

- Don't seek after riches or pleasures, or worry about life.
- Seek God with all your heart, mind, and soul, looking toward a rich, rewarding life now and certain eternal life later.

Remember this:

As long as the earth endures, seedtime and harvest ... will never cease (Genesis 8:22).

Whatever knowledge plants itself into your heart is seed. Now be careful. *"Do not be deceived: God cannot be mocked. A man reaps what he sows"* (Galatians 6:7).

Every seed produces after its own kind, so watch out for what seeds you allow to be planted in your heart. Things to which you **listen faithfully** will produce a crop. Don't let worldly seeds take root; plant only the Word of God in you. So, what are you listening to? Media? Radio? TV? News? If you are not careful, these things can be distractions that impede your development to true success. The fruit of worldly seed can lead to your destruction.

When a farmer wants a crop, he plants specific seed. Likewise, you need to plant seeds for your needs. Seeds you plant today will determine what you'll reap tomorrow.

Now, because Christ compared the Word of God to seed, then if there is a lack in your life of the things you desire, consider the principle of seedtime and harvest. Just keep hearing/planting and hearing/planting, and the power and force of God's Word will do the rest and produce a harvest in the proper season. Soon your areas of lack will be full.

Give, and it will be given to you. A good measure, pressed down, shaken together and running over, will be poured into your lap. For with the measure you use, it will be measured to you (Luke 6: 38).

YOU LACK	STUDY THE WORD OF GOD; SOW GOOD SEED
Love?	Give love to others whether they respond or not. (See Luke 6:35; 1 Corinthians 13.)
Finances?	Give food to the poor, give tithes and offerings, and/or bless someone financially. (See 1 Kings 2:3.)
Health?	Pray for others who are sick. Study healing scriptures, Christian books, tapes, sermons on healing. (See Matthew 9:35.)
Peace?	Pray for others to receive peace. Keep your mind on Jesus. (See Isaiah 26:3; Romans 8:6.)
Godly friends?	Be a friend to others, especially those you recognize as faithful to the Lord. Be cautious in friendship. (See Proverbs 12:26.)
Deliverance?	Pray for those with the same need. Do not be afraid, stand firm in the Lord. Seek godly counsel, books and pastoral advice. (See Exodus 14:13.)
Energy?	The Word is life—read it and speak it! Jesus came to give abundant life. (See John 10:10; Proverbs 10:4.)
Joy?	Lead a person to Jesus. There is joy in the heavens over one sinner that repents. Start praising the Lord. (See Luke 15:7; Isaiah 61:3.)

Don't worry about how your harvest will come to pass. Keep sowing godly seed! Continue faithfully listening and doing God's Word. He is the One who gives you the ability to produce!

> *Not that we are competent in ourselves to claim anything for ourselves, but our competence comes from God* (2 Corinthians 3:5).

> *He also said, "This is what the kingdom of God is like. A man scatters seed on the ground. Night and day, whether he sleeps or gets up, the seed sprouts and grows, though he does not know how. All by itself the soil produces grain—first the stalk, then the head, then the full kernel in the head. As soon as the grain is ripe, he puts the sickle to it, because the harvest has come"* (Mark 4:26-29).

Step up and prove yourself faithful right now, right where you are. Don't look down on your small beginnings. When you're faithful, even if it doesn't seem like much, God reveals the greatness of what you can become.

Dealing With Trials

It is so easy to tell you about how God is going to give you the victory. It is so easy because this is the will of our Father. When you go through trials, and you *will* go through trials, He has given you these words of comfort: *"When you pass through the waters, I will be with you; and when you pass through the rivers, they will not sweep over you. When you walk through the fire, you will not be burned; the flames will not set you ablaze"* (Isaiah 43:2).

Always keep this in mind: *"Many are the afflictions of the righteous: but the LORD delivereth him out of them all"* (Psalm 34:19, KJV). Oh, what a wonderful assurance of deliverance from the Lord. Keep on holding out. Keep on trusting and waiting.

Your being diligently patient is necessary to develop you into maturity. Maturity is the state where you come into the fullness of the promises. Understand this: God wants to bless you immensely, but you must be mature enough to handle the blessing. In order to reach maturity you must go through testing that will refine you and perfect you to what you will ultimately become.

How does a person develop his skills unless he exercises? How does a musician become proficient unless he practices? How does a dancer become better unless she dances? God uses the trials to exercise your faith. You may be confident of this: no matter what you go through, it will not overwhelm you. God has measured every trial and every resistance you have to face. He will not allow any more to come upon you than what you can bear, and when it does happen, He will provide a way out. Therefore, do not spend your time looking at or discussing the trial. Remember this is how your faith is weakened. Give satan no joy in your struggle; rather give God the praise. You don't have to wait until the battle is over to realize that you've already won. You can shout now.

So when you're going through hell on your job, in your family, in your school or wherever it may be, you can rest assured that God is developing you into a state that is greater than that in which you began. Consider these words: *"But we have this treasure in jars of clay to show that this all-surpassing power is from God and not from us. We are hard pressed on every side, but not crushed; perplexed, but not in despair"* (2 Corinthians 4:7-8).

At this point nothing can stop you. Keep this confidence: the longer you go through and remain faithful, being diligently patient and waiting on God, the greater the blessing.

How can I be confident of this? I have learned from the Word of God, and His Word is true. I have learned from those older and wiser than I who have seen much more than I have seen. May you learn from them also.

I was young and now I am old, yet I have never seen the righteous forsaken or their children begging bread (Psalm 37:25).

Therefore we do not lose heart. Though outwardly we are wasting away, yet inwardly we are being renewed day by day. For our light and momentary troubles are achieving for us an eternal glory that far outweighs them all. So we fix our eyes not on what is seen, but on what is unseen. For what is seen is temporary, but what is unseen is eternal (2 Corinthians 4:16-18).

Solomon had this to say regarding being diligent and patient: *"Go to the ant, you sluggard; consider its ways and be wise! It has no commander, no overseer or ruler, yet it stores its provisions in summer and gathers its food at harvest"* (Proverbs 6:6-8). He informs us that we have much to learn by examining even one of the smallest creatures that God has created. What can we learn from ants?

- They keep working even though you can destroy them with one footstep.
- They do not allow the threat of danger to stop them from the work they do.
- They work untiringly. They don't quit. Even if you step on their mound, they will come right back out and rebuild it.
- They perform all their jobs according to their ability.
- They work together in harmony. Although they are small, their unity allows them to do great works.
- When they get food, they take it back to share it with the others.
- They recognize their corporate potential to do more by working together than working individually.
- They do not need anyone to tell them what to do. If there is a job to be done, it is done.
- They do things for the good of the colony.
- They store their food, preparing for the future.

Lessons in Diligence

The Bible has much to say about diligence. Plans, no matter how good they sound or how detailed they might be, are just plans, until they're put into dynamic action. Your faith must be joined to your work. (See James 2:26.)

When trials and troubles come, don't put your plans on the back burner and allow discouragement and disappointment to take over your focus. Stay wisely on course.

Think about it. The wise and the foolish have the same number of hours in a day. How they use those hours proves their effectiveness in making progress toward a desired end. Ephesians 5:15-16 teaches us this principle: *"Be very careful, then, how you live—not as unwise but as wise, making the most of every opportunity."* Unfortunately, many Christians mistakenly think that because they believe in God, life should be an easy cakewalk. Nothing can be further from the truth. Even "the world" understands that accomplishing anything requires a measure of diligence.

Remember the fable about the tortoise and the hare? Let's use our imaginations for a moment. The crowds are standing around waiting to see a race. Many are pulling for the hare—they're just sure that he'll win the race. The tortoise doesn't allow the cheers from the crowd to deter him from reaching his goal. He must make it to the end. You know the story. The tortoise wins the race not because he's faster, but because he's diligently patient.

To receive the blessings of God takes effort! Hebrews 6:11 reads: *"We want each of you to show this same diligence to the very end, in order to make your hope sure."* Therefore, **finding it**, **aligning to it, inquiring of God**, and **taking action** are great steps. But to truly seize your God-given potential, you have to **hold out diligently**. This consistent pursuit daily moves you closer to the vision God has given you to reach your divine potential. Remember, it's not how big the steps are that's important. It's that you take the steps and continue to do so in order to complete the journey.

> *So do not throw away your confidence; it will be richly rewarded. You need to persevere so that when you have done the will of God, you will receive what he has promised* (Hebrews 10:35-36).

Seizing Your Divine Potential is a Process—Not an Event

Keep Ecclesiastes 9:11 in your view as you move forward on your journey: *"The race is not the swift or the battle to the strong ... "* Also, Matthew 10:22 assures us of the importance of our endurance and persistence: *"He who stands firm to the end will be saved."*

It will take time for you to seize your divine potential, but if you press on and continue in Christ, it will come to pass. God provides daily, not for weeks at a time.

- Moses was diligently patient and led the Israelites out of Egypt, but only after the ten trials or tests.
- Manna, the food from God, was provided daily.
- Joshua was diligently patient and circled the Jericho walls for seven days until there was victory.
- Samson defeated a thousand men with the jawbone of a donkey he found in a field just when he was about to do battle, not before. (Think about this: God had to have the donkey die at the right time and in the right place for Samson to find the jawbone.)

You can be confident that God has already provided the tools for your victory. The important thing for you to do is to be diligently patient and keep moving along progressively.

Develop persistent diligence to work out the plan to achieve your divine potential:

1. Realize that you only need to take each step one at a time. It took Jesus three years to complete His mission on earth. It'll take you some time to accomplish God's divine purpose and plan in you.

2. Don't allow your efforts to become hindrances. Remember, the effort it takes to achieve your divine potential will prove worthwhile at the proper season. Galatians 6:9 clearly reads, *"Let us not become weary in doing good, for at the proper time we will reap a harvest if we do not give up."*

3. Develop a tolerance for short-term discomfort as you journey toward your long-term destination in God.

4. Make no excuses. Put nothing off for later. Soon, later becomes longer and longer, until it becomes never.

5. Be casual about momentary setbacks. Paul provided this encouragement in Philippians 3:13-14: *"Brethren, I count not myself to have apprehended: but this one thing I do, forgetting those things which are behind, and reaching forth unto those things which are before, I press toward the mark for the prize of the high calling of*

God in Christ Jesus." Remember, the greater the sacrifice you make to achieve God's purposes, the greater the rewards.

6. Be mentally tough and continuously study to fill yourself with the knowledge of who you are. You're created in His image and likeness and blessed with endless empowerment and with a divine directive to be fruitful, multiply, replenish, and subdue the earth, and to have dominion over all things in the earth, seen and unseen.

7. Commit yourself to reaching the place God desires for you to be: the place of your original design. Commit to achieving your divine potential.

8. Be persistent in your prayer life so that you won't faint. (See Luke 18:1.)

9. Persevere to the end, knowing that God's purposes and plans for you shall not fail.

So much can be said regarding being diligently patient. Keep pressing on. Keep holding out. Now, one final word:

> *Do you not know? Have you not heard? The Lord is the everlasting God, the Creator of the ends of the earth. He will not grow tired or weary, and his understanding no one can fathom. He gives strength to the weary and increases the power of the weak. Even youths grow tired and weary, and young men stumble and fall; but those who hope in the Lord will renew their strength. They will soar on wings like eagles; they will run and not grow weary, they will walk and not be faint* (Isaiah 40:28-31).

YOUR DIVINE POTENTIAL POWER POINTS

1. Rejoice in all that you've accomplished toward achieving your divine potential.

2. Be determined to work out the plan God has given you. Fill yourself with the knowledge of:

- Who you are
- Where you are
- God's purpose for your life
- Your plan

3. Keep the end in mind (even if you can't foresee the outcome) and work your plan one step at a time.

4. Be diligently patient to seize your divine potential in spite of obstacles and hindrances.

Are you faithful in the little things?

- Prove yourself faithful and true here at your current level right now.
- What you'll become is not dependent on what you have now, but on how you use it.

Are you faithful to listen to the Word of God?
- Consider carefully how you listen—
    - Perceive by your senses: see, feel, and hear the Word of God.
    - Discern mentally: observe, perceive, discover, and understand the Word of God.
    - Turn your thoughts or direct your mind to the Word of God: consider, contemplate, look at, and weigh carefully through examination.
    - Discover by use: understand the Word of God by putting it into action.
- **Faithfully listen** to the Word of God—your seed.
- What are you listening to?
- Watch out for the seeds you allow to be planted in your heart.
- Plant seeds for your needs. If you have a need, plant a seed.

Write from your heart a prayer asking God to strengthen you in your weaknesses, to take control of your will by the power of His Spirit, and to give you spiritual ears to really listen to His voice:

_____

_____

_____

_____

_____

_____

_____

As Paul prayed for the Colossians, I pray this Scripture for you now.

Since the day we heard about you, we haven't stopped praying for you and asking God to fill you with the knowledge of His will through all spiritual wisdom and understanding. And we pray this in order that you may live a life worthy of the Lord and may please Him in every way: bearing fruit in every good work, growing in the knowledge of God, being strengthened with all power according to His glorious might so that you may have great endurance and patience, and joyfully giving thanks to the Father, who has qualified you to share in the inheritance of the saints in the kingdom of light (Colossians 1:9-10).

CHAPTER 10

A Final Word

The Other Side of Seizing Your Divine Potential

Look back at the five performance principles you have studied:

1. Find Out Who You Are,
2. Align Yourself With the Word of God,
3. Inquire of God About Your Divine Potential,
4. Take Action to Achieve Your Divine Potential, and
5. Hold out and Be Diligently Patient.

Each one of these performance principles assists you in growing in the Word of God. As you grow in the Word of God, you grow in faith. As you grow in faith, you grow in favor with God. As you grow in favor, you experience the power of His anointing in your life. It is His anointing that destroys the yoke of oppression and mediocrity that has too long enslaved many of us. You were created to be free and to glorify God with your life. You are the salt of the earth and the light of the world. God desires for you to shine and to preserve His image and His likeness in the world.

You will maintain a righteous life as you diligently study and progressively move along the path to your divine potential. The more the Word is in you, the more it purges that within you which is undesirable to God. I have tried to connect the dots—the areas of the Word of God that will lead you to your divine potential. If you take the time to review again and again and meditate upon the principles that have been established, you will find ever-increasing peace in your life and confidence of knowing that all things are being worked out together for your good.

The more I have lived my life and waited on God, the more I have seen God deliver every time. There are times in which I may ponder my deliverance and its timing, but I am certain that I will be delivered. The same is true with you. The more you study, the more confident you will become that God will deliver you from the difficulty you are encountering. With this certainty you will know that the divine potential in you will be achieved and the world will be changed by Christ who is in you.

It is truly an honor to be used by God. You rejoice at knowing that He thought you worthy enough to invest His power in you. The principal fact that He has chosen to dwell in you causes you to face each day with great excitement. You are eager to know how God will manifest His presence in you to accomplish great exploits for the benefit of the world through you. How blessed you are!

As you allow Him to use you as an instrument of His anointing, you are blessed by the overflow of His blessings to others. You receive what you have no fear of losing. You are blessed in ways that no man or demon can take away. The results of your submission to His will to develop your divine potential assure you a rich welcome into the eternal Kingdom of our Lord and Savior Jesus.

From this day onward, you understand that God's will for your life is progressive. He will see you on to completion and to the fulfillment of your divine potential. You can achieve it. You do not have to be concerned if you haven't grasped it all yet. You understand that all you have to do is be persistently diligent in applying yourself to the greater knowledge of His Word daily. You know that God works in you to bring to pass His will for your life. All you have to do is continue to present your body as a living sacrifice before Him each day. (See Romans 12:1.)

As you continue to serve Him and to walk as blamelessly as you can, He reveals His will to you day by day. Therefore, take one day at a time. Don't worry about next week, but apply yourself to the work that is present before you this day. God will be with you next week and will give you what you need when you need it. He has taught us to pray, "Give us this day our *daily* bread." He has taught us that when the manna came from Heaven in the wilderness, it was just enough for one day. As it has always been, so shall it also be with you. God will provide daily for whatever you need.

This will require effort and more effort and then more effort, but the results will certainly prove that our labor has not been in vain. Keep on in faith with persistent diligence and remain diligently patient. As you continue in Him, God reveals His will to you step by step. Take each step as it comes! Follow the Lord steadfastly until you leave this world to go to be with your Father in Heaven. There's no death for you—only life on earth and then life in Heaven.

Press Onward. Don't Quit!

Develop your tolerance for short-term discomfort. Anything that is of value will cost you something. Do not let the estimated cost discourage you from pressing on. There will be times when you will be challenged. You will be tired, but keep looking toward the end. You will have to sacrifice in order to gain, but your sacrifice demonstrates your faith and your faith will be rewarded by God.

If you're going to make it to the destination God has for you, you must resist the temptation to become discouraged or doubtful because of setbacks. Do not be discouraged as a result of life's challenges; rather, welcome them as opportunities to develop into perfection.

> *Brethren, I count not myself to have apprehended: but this one thing I do, forgetting those things which are behind, and reaching forth unto those things which are before, I press toward the mark for the prize of the high calling of God in Christ Jesus* (Philippians 3:13-14, KJV).

Remember that the greater the sacrifice you make to achieve God's purposes, the greater the rewards. Keep your eyes on the "prize of the high calling" and the eternal riches in Heaven above.

Persevere to the end, knowing that God didn't bring you this far to leave you. Weeping may endure for a night, but joy comes in the morning. You have the certainty of your victory. It is guaranteed by the Creator of the universe who never fails. Be "...confident of this, that he who began a good work in you will carry it on to completion until the day of Christ Jesus" (Philippians 1:6).

We want each of you to show this same diligence to the very end, in order to make your hope sure. We do not want you to become lazy, but to imitate those who through faith and patience inherit what has been promised (Hebrews 6:11-12).

One Step Closer!

Daily move ever closer to the vision God has given you, even if it's a small step. Diligence counts!

"I have seen something else under the sun: The race is not to the swift or the battle to the strong, nor does food come to the wise or wealth to the brilliant or favor to the learned; but time and chance happen to them all" (Ecclesiastes 9:11).

Prepare and pace yourself to go the distance. Throughout your race, cast your cares upon God. Learn to be content in each moment, knowing victory is at the end. You may not win today, but in the end, you will win.

Allow the divine potential to manifest itself in you. God has a vision and a mission for you to accomplish. It is greater than you. It is greater than anything you have ever imagined. Indeed, you are not capable of achieving it alone, but the provision is in the potential, so focus on your divine potential. Your potential will manifest the provision at the right time.

Though you may be faced with physical limitations, these by no means affect your divine potential. God knew your physical handicaps before you were born. Your divine potential is not based upon your ability, but upon His. Additionally, your divine potential for greatness is not limited by education, race, economic status, or any natural impediment. It is set and established by the spiritual effect of God's Word. Therefore, do not become discouraged at your present station in life. It has no bearing on what your tomorrow can become.

I want to share with you two more encouraging events that are recorded in scripture. The first involves an event in the life of Elijah in a little town called Zarephath. There was a famine in the land and the Lord told him to go to the town because He had commanded a widow there to provide food for him. Please understand that this widow really had no food:

So he went to Zarephath. When he came to the town gate, a widow was there gathering sticks. He called to her and asked, "Would you bring me a little water in a jar so I may have a drink?" As she was going to get it, he called, "And bring me, please, a piece of bread."

"As surely as the Lord your God lives," she replied, "I don't have any bread—only a handful of flour in a jar and a little oil in a jug. I am gathering a few sticks to take home and make a meal for myself and my son, that we may eat it—and die."

Elijah said to her, "Don't be afraid. Go home and do as you have said. But first make a small cake of bread for me from what you have and bring it to me, and then make something for yourself and your son. For this is what the Lord, the God of Israel, says: 'The jar of flour will not be used up and the jug of oil will not run dry until the day the Lord gives rain on the land.'"

She went away and did as Elijah had told her. So there was food every day for Elijah and for the woman and her family. For the jar of flour was not used up and the jug of oil did not run dry, in keeping with the word of the Lord spoken by Elijah (1 Kings 17:10-16, emphasis mine).

Now the second story:

> *The wife of a man from the company of the prophets cried out to Elisha, "Your servant my husband is dead, and you know that he revered the Lord. But now his creditor is coming to take my two boys as his slaves." Elisha replied to her, "How can I help you? Tell me, what do you have in your house?" "Your servant has nothing there at all," she said, "except a little oil." Elisha said, "Go around and ask all your neighbors for empty jars. Don't ask for just a few. Then go inside and shut the door behind you and your sons. Pour oil into all the jars, and as each is filled, put it to one side."*
>
> *She left him and afterward shut the door behind her and her sons. They brought the jars to her and she kept pouring.* **When all the jars were full,** *she said to her son, "Bring me another one." But he replied, "There is not a jar left."* **Then the oil stopped flowing.** *She went and told the man of God, and he said, "Go, sell the oil and pay your debts. You and your sons can live on what is left"* (2 Kings 4:1-7, emphasis mine).

Now, please learn the lesson of these two stories. Both women assumed they had nothing. Their condition in the natural indeed looked bleak. However, the "nothing" they had was full of potential. The Word of God, spoken from God's man, took the little they had and extracted the full potential from it. For one, it was a handful of flour and a little oil. For the other, it was just a little oil. But a little was all the Word of God needed to fulfill a great need.

Such is the case with you. The divine potential is there. Let God's Word reveal it in you. Life is driven by choice. Where you go from here is your choice.

My prayer is that God will touch you, as He has touched me to have the confidence of knowing that you, too, can achieve your divine potential.

May "the Lord bless you and keep you;
The Lord make His face to shine upon you and be gracious
unto you;
The Lord turn his face toward you and give you peace"
(Numbers 6:24-26).

In the mighty name of Jesus I pray!
God bless you!